Crash Course in Basic Cataloging
with RDA

Crash Course in Basic Cataloging with RDA

Heather Lea Moulaison and Raegan Wiechert

Crash Course

LIBRARIES
UNLIMITED™

An Imprint of ABC-CLIO, LLC

Santa Barbara, California • Denver, Colorado

Library of Congress Cataloging-in-Publication Data

Moulaison, Heather Lea, author.
  Crash course in basic cataloging with RDA / Heather Lea Moulaison and Raegan Wiechert.
    pages cm. — (Crash course)
  Includes bibliographical references and index.
    ISBN 978-1-4408-3776-0 (paperback) — ISBN 978-1-4408-3777-7 (ebook)
1. Cataloging.   2. Resource description & access.   3. Classification—Books.
I. Wiechert, Raegan, author.   II. Title.
  Z693.M68   2015
  025.3'2—dc23   2015017302

ISBN: 978-1-4408-3776-0
EISBN: 978-1-4408-3777-7

19 18 17 16 15   1 2 3 4 5

This book is also available on the World Wide Web as an eBook.
Visit www.abc-clio.com for details.

Libraries Unlimited
An Imprint of ABC-CLIO, LLC

ABC-CLIO, LLC
130 Cremona Drive, P.O. Box 1911
Santa Barbara, California 93116-1911

This book is printed on acid-free paper ∞

Manufactured in the United States of America

CONTENTS

ILLUSTRATIONS

FIGURES

SIDEBARS

TABLES

INTRODUCTION

Cataloging is an integral part of library operations. At the most basic level, libraries must have content, and beyond that, the content must be organized. There are many, many other services libraries offer, but fundamentally, at the heart of it, a library is not a library if it does not provide access to organized content.

Cataloging is how library content is organized. Cataloging is carried out in technical services departments or in other behind-the-scenes operations. Larger libraries might have an entire Cataloging Department as part of its Technical Services unit with fleets of catalogers at the ready, each specialized in a certain area. This book, while a welcome refresher for them perhaps, is not designed for those librarians.

Instead, this *Crash Course* is intended for librarians and library employees who are not experts and who are left to work through the intricacies of cataloging with little professional guidance. Here, we approach current cataloging from a practical standpoint for *non-catalogers*. Understanding elements of the cataloging process and record and being able to interact with records in a basic way is the primary focus of this book.

Of course, not all readers will have the same background or the same purpose in picking up this book. Some might be interested in cross-training and might already be working with library technology or in library administration; others might find themselves suddenly responsible for a library's cataloging and need to find a reasonable point of departure for carrying out their work. Students taking Cataloging at the associate or master's level will be able to use this book as a practical supplement to their course books; additionally, courses in Technical Services librarianship or Organization of Information at the master's level might find it a useful textbook for the "Cataloging" module.

This little guide is an up-to-date resource that will enable those interested in cataloging, but who do not come to it with a weighty cataloging background, to understand cataloging in the current RDA environment. With the advent of new web technologies, all aspects of cataloging are rapidly evolving, and new thinking is required. New terms, new tools, and new approaches have also followed the adoption of the content standard, RDA, and this book gives an overview to all of them for those starting out.

HOW TO READ THIS BOOK

This book features the kind of information needed to be successful in practical cataloging. We recommend you read it through once, skimming if that makes the most sense. There is a lot here, so you might want to let it sink in a little.

Then, we suggest you go back and reread the parts that are most relevant to what you are trying to accomplish. We supply ample references and resources, many of which are web-based and free. Check out the references and resources associated with the chapters that are the most relevant. All of this reading and surfing will take a fair amount of time on your part, and that is okay. The standard wisdom around libraries used to be that it took three years to learn how to catalog and five years to have it make sense. Please understand that this is a journey, and picking up this book is one of the best ways to have started.

One recommendation, which you may choose to accept or reject, is to work at a computer with the largest screen you can find. In many large libraries, librarians working in the cataloging department were among the first to be outfitted with dual-monitor workstations. This was no accident. In order to catalog correctly, a number of different resources need to be consulted, and many of them are online.

STRUCTURE OF THE BOOK

This book is organized into 10 chapters. We begin by setting the stage for the cataloging task, then describe the tasks carried out during the cataloging process, and finally situate them in terms of their place in making information available to patrons.

In Chapter 1, we address the big-picture issues in cataloging. We are assuming that you come to this with no background at all in the area, so we give you a bit of a foundation and permit you to understand some of the basic context for cataloging, including the roles of the Library of Congress (LC) and the background to the current cataloging instructions, Resource Description and Access (RDA). We also describe some of the basic notions that are essential to cataloging, including the importance of doing things the same way from library to library in order to enable libraries to share cataloging records.

In Chapter 2, we talk about the computer systems that house and display cataloging records. Standards for encoding are important, and the computer systems, called integrated library systems (ILSs), are where the rubber hits the road. Librarians use these systems to store cataloging records, and patrons use them or more user-friendly interfaces, to search for those records. This chapter also addresses issues of how the catalog is searched, and how local practice might be taken into consideration when cataloging.

Chapter 3 describes different formats and approaches that will affect cataloging. ebooks and traditional print books may be identical, but if users do not have access to a computerized e-reading device or system, only the print book will be of interest to them. This chapter looks at differences for fiction and nonfiction and juvenile and adult materials. Although RDA helps us describe and create access points for all materials, it is helpful to understand what some unique characteristics of different materials might be. This chapter sets the stage for the different discussions in the RDA chapters and in the processing chapter, Chapter 10.

In Chapter 4, we get down to brass tacks in describing MARC, Machine-Readable Cataloging. MARC is complex, and, until present, has stood the test of time. MARC may not be web-ready, but it is what libraries use right now to encode their cataloging records, and it is important to understand the big picture of what MARC is and can do. You will also want to look at Appendix A for a number of examples of MARC records.

Toward the end of Chapter 4, we describe some alternative approaches to encoding library data and update you on how potential changes to MARC and to the way the web works will affect libraries in the future. Although they will probably not affect the cataloging you do today, they will likely have an impact on the field in the years to come.

In the chapters on RDA, Chapters 5 and 6, we discuss everything you need to know to get your hands dirty with RDA. In the process, we provide you with loads of examples, encoded in MARC, to get you started. You will want to look at Appendix A as you flip through, even if we do not specifically tell you to, so that you can see these fields in the context of a number of examples.

In Chapter 7, we describe RDA access points, yet another value-added aspect that catalogers supply in cataloging records to promote retrieval. Access points can be created for authors, for example, as well as for titles. This allows the catalog to pull together works by an author who changes his or her name in a way Amazon cannot dream of replicating.

Chapter 8 describes subject headings in library cataloging. Subject headings are compiled in lists, and it is up to the cataloger to choose the correct term for the item when cataloging. Library of Congress Subject Headings (LCSH) are the most commonly used, and we describe them in a fair bit of detail. We also mention a few other lists that your library might be using, and compare them briefly to LCSH.

In Chapter 9, we focus on library classification using two of the most common classification schemes, Dewey Decimal Classification (DDC), known by most as Dewey, and Library of Congress Classification (LCC). We also break down the parts of a call number and explain them, describing how and why call numbers look the way they do.

The last chapter, Chapter 10, talks about the practical aspects of bringing cataloging records into a library system. How can records be acquired? Where can records be purchased in bulk? What might a standard cataloging workflow entail? What kind of processing should you expect for different kinds of materials, including audio-visual? How might the final check be carried out? We answer these questions, and provide lists of elements to consider along the way.

As mentioned, there are appendices at the end of this book. Just because this content is outside of the regular chapters does not mean it is less important or less relevant to cataloging! In fact, the resources and examples you will find there will be instrumental in helping you answer questions that fall outside the scope of this book.

The first appendix, Appendix A, shows two sets of examples. First, you will find seven MARC records illustrative of the concepts we have been describing in the book, taken from LC. Although reading records might not be the most fun way to spend an afternoon, it will help you become familiar with a somewhat complex encoding scheme.

In the second part of Appendix A, we provide the RDA rules for those same seven resources' content. Where in RDA do we learn what to provide in the MARC 245? Just flip from the MARC record to the RDA record to see how catalogers know where to find content. In the RDA section, we have color-coded the fields. The white fields are required, according to RDA. The others are not, but catalogers include them and we highly recommend that you do too.

The second appendix, Appendix B, is primarily a webliography of useful resources for cataloging. It is worth it to take the time to check them out. We do mention quite a few of them in the course of the book, but this appendix gives us the opportunity to mention even more resources and to organize them to give them some additional context. We also provide some non-web references, such as books and journals, that will help support you as you become more proficient in cataloging with RDA.

Finally, the third appendix, Appendix C, lists and describes networks and resources for connecting with the cataloging community and learning more deeply about topics. The standards and practices that support cataloging change regularly, and it is a good idea to know what is being discussed and what advances and new technologies are on the horizon. The resources we list here will help you do just that.

CONCLUSION

As cataloging standards are changing with the evolution of content, the job of the cataloger is also changing. Information professionals working with cataloging records may not need to create them but will need to understand the records they have. A basic understanding of all elements of current cataloging practice is important: cataloging records, the cataloging environment, the work of the cataloger, the cataloger's tools, and current practice. It is not necessary to have followed every advance over the past 10 years in order to understand the basics of cataloging today. While not a definitive guide to doing all parts of cataloging, this book will, however, explain just enough to make you "dangerous."

We applaud you for taking the steps to acquire this book and wish you Happy Cataloging!

CHAPTER 1

What Is Cataloging?

In a book about cataloging, it makes sense to start by defining what cataloging is. *Cataloging* means describing and providing access to library materials through the use of recognized standards. Catalogers describe what the physical (or electronic) container is like, supply names of authors and subjects in a systematic way, and, in the case of physical objects, prepare them for discovery and retrieval through assigning a shelf location, in many cases a call number using Dewey Decimal Classification (DDC) or Library of Congress Classification (LCC).

All of this descriptive and subject-based information about materials exists only because catalogers organize and create it—catalogers must type out information, often by hand, and use recognized markup languages such as MARC (Machine-Readable Cataloging) in order to have that information understood by their library computer systems. Using consistent markup languages and standards permits libraries to exchange electronic cataloging information easily, potentially saving someone down the line some additional work.

For example, Library A can catalog an item, and if another library, Library B, acquires an identical item, the cataloging information can be shared as an electronic file called a catalog record; in this book, we also call electronic files about materials *cataloging records* and *bibliographic records*. Since it is impossible to add physical objects to a database, the best catalogers can do is to create and provide access to these catalog records (also known as *surrogates* in the library literature) that will stand in for the actual object, allowing users to know if a collection contains the materials they want.

When in the scenario described above, Library B downloads Library A's electronic catalog record for use in its own local catalog, that is known as *copy cataloging*. We will talk about copy cataloging later in this chapter (see especially Sidebar 1.1), but for now,

1

understand that copy cataloging is when one library takes another library's record and, perhaps with slight modifications, uses it in its local system. If the library where you work acquires materials that are held in other libraries, then you too will be doing copy cataloging if you use another library's record as a point of departure in your cataloging. And, to do your modifications well, you will need to understand some basic notions about cataloging.

The way we think of cataloging in this book is consistent with the definitions presented in cataloging textbooks and with generally accepted definitions used in librarianship.[1] We, like others, think that cataloging is essential—it is one of the pillars of library science, and without it there is no access.

Why is cataloging so important? Because without it, library users will not know what a library has and will not be able to access the materials, be they print, A/V, web-based, and so on. Indeed, electronic content may be increasingly ubiquitous, but if not uniformly described and made searchable, none of the content in libraries stands a chance at being discovered. If potential users do not know what the library has, they are unlikely to become actual users.

If libraries want potential users to become actual, satisfied users who make use of their collections, the cataloging process needs to be understood and appreciated. With the exception of physical processing (discussed in Chapter 10), cataloging is based on the application of standards. These standards are agreed upon by a number of national and international bodies. Individual libraries are not *required* to follow these standards, but most do follow them because they allow for easier sharing of information about library resources between and among libraries, that is, copy cataloging.

STANDARDS IN THE UNITED STATES

Standards are around us all the time. Three-hole punches need to be calibrated to match the holes in 3-hole binders. Barcode readers need to be adapted to the kind of code in use. Standards can be applied at the local or institution-specific level, among a group of institutions, or formally at a national or international level.

Libraries may decide on *local practice* as a way of consistently approaching a situation in a way that is adapted to their users' needs; this might also happen at the cluster or group level when a number of libraries adopt identical sets of *best practices*. In the United States, the non-profit American National Standards Institute (ANSI) (often pronounced *antsy*) is concerned with U.S.-based standards in all sectors; its mission is to promote and facilitate *voluntary consensus standards*. At present, work with standards relating to libraries and information are overseen by the ANSI-created nonprofit National Information Standards Organization (NISO) (pronounced *nigh-so*). NISO has been the institution responsible for the standards beginning with Z39, such as the Z39.50 protocol (see Chapter 10 for more information), and in fact, the entire organization was known as Z39 until 1984 and not accredited by ANSI until 1987[2].

Practice can go from local to national to international over time as communities decide that it is right. For example, the Library of Congress created MARC, the encoding standard used in library cataloging. The standard was first codified nationally in the United States. Later, when MARC became international, it was codified by the international body, the International Organization for Standardization (ISO), as ISO 2709. MARC, which started in Washington D.C., is now formally used in libraries around the world.

"How long can it take to put a spine label on and move the book to the shelf?" may be the cry of exasperated patrons wanting library items before they can be fully processed. There is much more to cataloging than slapping a spine label on a book, however, and librarians and administrators alike need to understand and appreciate the work that cataloging entails, along with the benefits that it brings. Although this extra time can seem like an eternity to an impatient patron, it is what creates organization out of what would otherwise be absolute chaos. Cataloging makes a library's carefully curated collections usable.

MODERN CATALOGING

In the late 1800s, Charles Ammi Cutter formulated rules for a *dictionary catalog,* a kind of card catalog popular at the time. Although his rules have been revised and expanded upon by a number of others, the basic theory behind the rules is still upheld today. Cutter enumerated three *objects*, or objectives, for the catalog. These are shown in Figure 1.1 as they appeared in the 1904 edition of his work.

OBJECTS.*

1. To enable a person to find a book of which either
   (A) the author
   (B) the title   is known.
   (c) the subject
2. To show what the library has
   (D) by a given author
   (E) on a given subject
   (F) in a given kind of literature.
3. To assist in the choice of a book
   (G) as to its edition (bibliographically).
   (H) as to its character (literary or topical).

Figure 1.1 Cutter's Objects.[3]

What do all of these really mean? What is the catalog supposed to be? It might be easier to start with what it is not: the library catalog is not intended to contain everything but the kitchen sink in terms of data about library materials. It is instead designed to assist users with known-item searches of a library's holdings. For example, if a patron knows which author he or she wants to read, the catalog better be able to tell him or her if the library has a book by that author.

Specifically, the catalog must contain the information necessary to retrieve the records for the appropriate materials in the library's collection. The catalog enables users to find a library's materials by author, title, or subject (finding function); to pull together all a library's materials based on these same criteria (author, title, subject) (collocation function); and, based on additional information provided in the cataloging record, to understand if the material will meet their needs (evaluation function). These were ambitious goals in the age of paper retrieval systems, and they serve as the underlying structure for library catalogs today.

More recently, user tasks adapted to the electronic world in which we live and work have been elaborated. The *Functional Requirements for Bibliographic Records* (FRBR) (1998) (see further explanation that follows) *user tasks* were developed as part of the thought process exploring the content that truly needs to be included in each catalog record. What do users want to do? Having established these tasks, librarians could then give thought to the contents of catalog records that will meet those needs. The four user tasks FRBR identified are:

1. to *find* entities that correspond to the user's stated search criteria (i.e., to locate either a single entity or a set of entities in a file or database as the result of a search using an attribute or relationship of the entity);

2. to *identify* an entity (i.e., to confirm that the entity described corresponds to the entity sought, or to distinguish between two or more entities with similar characteristics);

3. to *select* an entity that is appropriate to the user's needs (i.e., to choose an entity that meets the user's requirements with respect to content, physical format, and so on, or to reject an entity as being inappropriate to the user's needs);

4. to acquire or *obtain* access to the entity described (i.e., to acquire an entity through purchase, loan, etc., or to access an entity electronically through an online connection to a remote computer).[4]

An additional user task was identified by Elaine Svenonius (2000): that of *navigate*. Navigate is especially critical in the modern electronic context. Library catalogs are great at allowing patrons to search; however, they are not fundamentally designed to permit navigating the same way that web resources do. The library world is moving in that direction, and the additional user task of navigate has the potential to situate the catalog at the cutting edge of new web-based technologies. Throughout it all, the point of the catalog has been and continues to be to make sure users can know what a library has, so that they can decide whether or not it has what they need.

RULES AND RULE MAKERS

Cataloging is about following rules to provide access in a consistent way with the goal of allowing patrons to access library materials. Who exactly is in charge of making all of these rules? In the United States, it is primarily the Library of Congress (LC) along with its partners such as the American Library Association (ALA) and libraries taking part in the Program for Cooperative Cataloging (PCC).

In 1901, LC started to sell catalog cards. This was a wonderful step for U.S.-based libraries, as it allowed them to use cataloging *copy* created by the most prestigious library in the country (see Sidebar 1.1). This copy cataloging was a great help, a fantastic alternative to each library doing its own cataloging, or possibly not to having any cataloging at all. However, it also meant that, for consistency, libraries cataloged according to LC's rules. Although many U.S.-based libraries still follow most of LC's rules today, the only librarians *required* to follow them are LC's employees. Everyone else is free to make decisions about what is best for their users locally.

SIDEBAR 1.1   TERMINOLOGY ALERT: COPY CATALOGING/ ORIGINAL CATALOGING

An important concept in cataloging is whether the cataloger is creating the catalog record or simply adapting it. It is generally better to avoid creating records from scratch if possible. Catalogers prefer to save some work and take advantage of someone else's records when they can. Below, we define two terms related to this idea that will show up throughout this book.

Copy cataloging: Checking, possibly adapting, and using a catalog record that someone else created. Most of the cataloging that is done by public and school libraries is copy cataloging since the books these libraries acquire are not unique or exotic.

Original cataloging: Creating a catalog record from scratch. If the item being cataloged is not held anywhere else, the library with the item will need to create a record to provide access.

Aside from providing general cataloging rules, LC also provides guidance for organizing materials based on what the materials are about and maintains controlled vocabularies, or specialized and maintained lists of terms, for providing access. LC devised and maintains a list of subject headings called the Library of Congress Subject Headings (LCSH) (see Chapter 8). As of January 2015, LCSH estimates that its list has 337,354 terms.[5] Most American and many international libraries use LCSH because of its wide availability, high quality, and good reputation. LC also maintains genre headings that describe what an item is: Library of Congress Genre/Form Terms for Library and Archival Materials (LCGFT). LC has also developed its own classification schedules (LCC) for organizing materials on its own shelves. LC is primarily a research library, so it stands to reason that the classification system it maintains would appeal more to research and academic libraries. Indeed, the overwhelming majority of U.S. public and school libraries use the Dewey Decimal Classification (DDC) to organize their materials. In addition, LC maintains a list of authorized name headings so that authors' names, for example, will be supplied consistently from library to library (discussed further in Chapter 7). This list of names is freely available online for anyone to use.

Internationally, the International Federation of Library Associations and Institutions (IFLA) has done much work with the theory of bibliographic organization. In 1998, it published FRBR. Rather than being a specific set of rules, FRBR is a conceptual model for library organizations like LC to base rules upon. FRBR is part thought-experiment, part roadmap. It is the product of an IFLA working group that, over a period of several years, explored the problem of what cataloging records need to do. FRBR is freely available online and is surprisingly readable.[6]

A Short History of Recent Cataloging Rules

Cataloging rules and instructions guide in the creation of descriptive cataloging elements. Without rules, it would be impossible for librarians in different libraries to describe the physical attributes of materials identically. It would also be impossible to write out the names of persons, for example, in a way that would be consistent. Descriptive cataloging governed by the rules does not describe how to classify materials or where to place an item on the shelf, but it does help patrons understand what is being described.

Many catalogers today have known only one or two generations of cataloging rules. In 1978, *Anglo-American Cataloguing Rules*, second edition (AACR2), was published and was adopted shortly thereafter. These AACR2 rules were revised in 1988 and 1998 and then revised and republished to become a loose-leaf publication with yearly updates in 2002. The Joint Steering Committee for Revision of AACR (JSC) was the body responsible for making revisions and additions to AACR2. At the time, members of the JSC came from organizations based in the United States, Canada, the United Kingdom, and Australia, and included representatives from LC and ALA.[7] In 2004, the JSC decided to revise AACR2 extensively and in December 2004, the draft part I of AACR3 was put out for review.

In 2005, however, the JSC decided to scrap AACR3 completely and start fresh in a totally different direction. The draft of the first part of Resource Description and Access (RDA) was made available in November 2005, with further drafts issued in 2006 and 2007. It was at this time that the JSC changed its name to the Joint Steering Committee for Development of RDA (JSC).[8] Finally, in 2008 a full draft was made available. Although RDA was published in 2010, it underwent a period of testing, with formal adoption put off until March 31, 2013.

All this being said, there are no requirements from the ALA or any other governing body forcing libraries to use RDA. A number of institutions, including LC, however, are requiring their employees to use RDA. Since LC is still responsible for a large portion of copy cataloging records, most libraries are going ahead and switching to RDA because it is easier to accept copy that way. Also, libraries are under no obligation to "update" any AACR2 records to RDA standards, but they can if desired. Remaining close to modern cataloging practice has its advantages, and as vendors update their products to work with RDA records, libraries with only AACR2 records may find themselves left behind.

RDA is not intended to be cataloging *rules*, but to be cataloging *instructions*. When originally conceived, it was designed to be an online-only product. However, many institutions argued that their budget would not allow for yearly subscription costs and RDA was made available in print. Online, RDA instructions are accessible through the RDA Toolkit (http://toolkit.rda.com). The Toolkit is a searchable and browseable database that is described in more detail in Chapter 5 of this book. The Toolkit also includes access to other resources, like MARC to RDA mappings and customizable workflows.

TEN-SECOND TIP: HOW TO TELL THE DIFFERENCE BETWEEN RDA AND AACR2 AT A GLANCE

In copy cataloging, it is likely you will run across old AACR2 records, so you will need to know what they are when you see them. One of the most noticeable differences at a glance is that AACR2 records will have abbreviations for pages (p.), edition (ed.), and illustrations (ill.). RDA records (generally) do not have any abbreviations. There will be other differences as well that may look wrong for someone used to dealing with RDA, such as missing information about the content's carrier and different information about the publication of the item. AACR2 records, however, are not wrong; they just were created through the use of a different set of instructions.

Sharable Records

Catalogers create records for patrons to use, but if information is not consistently and correctly supplied, retrieval cannot be guaranteed. Quality is therefore a major concern when it comes to catalog records. The work done by the cataloger facilitates access to the library's materials, and if done correctly and consistently, patrons will be able to find all the library's materials meeting their criteria through the use of the catalog (see further discussion about the catalog in Chapter 2).

As mentioned, one of the main aims of professional cataloging is the creation of records that permit access and conform to a set of standards. By providing high-quality records, a library's own patrons can find materials. Especially for local or unique materials, it becomes necessary for libraries to do original cataloging, that is, create brand-new records for materials they have (revisit Sidebar 1.1). Once a record is created, any institution can use it—if the item it describes is acquired and if the record for the item can be found and uploaded. Like a good laugh or even a smile, catalog records are best shared.

Unlike creative intellectual property that is copyrighted, catalog records are a kind of recorded acknowledgement of the physical and intellectual characteristics of materials. Catalogers sometimes claim that cataloging is more of an art than a science, but from an intellectual property point of view, cataloging is a faithful description of a material's characteristics. For this reason, like the information found in phone books or other public records, the information in catalog records is factual. Since copyright only applies to creative works, it is generally safe to consider that records can be shared—especially if the records are made freely available. For example, when libraries participate in LC's Gateway to Library Catalogs (http://www.loc.gov/z3950/) for record-sharing, it is okay to assume they want other libraries to have access to their cataloging records for copy cataloging purposes. When records adhere to current standards, their usefulness is guaranteed in a maximum of additional institutions.

CONCLUSION

In this chapter, we set the stage for the importance of cataloging. Cataloging is one of the pillars of modern librarianship, and current practices are rooted in tried-and-true traditional approaches. Even though a library is not required to provide some kinds of access, there is a definite benefit in doing what everyone else is doing: in following standards. Standards permit interoperability, which is import not only for the present but also for the future. Even libraries that are independent today may be part of a shared cataloging network in the future. Given that the future is longer than the past, now is an excellent time to make sure that your library's practices conform to national standards! The following chapters will guide you in that process.

NOTES

1. Arlene G. Taylor. 2006. *Introduction to Cataloging and Classification*. With David P. Miller. Tenth edition. Westport, Connecticut: Libraries Unlimited; Reitz, Joan M. "Cataloging." *ODLIS: Online Dictionary for Library and Information Science*. 2014. http://www.abc-clio.com/ODLIS/odlis_c.aspx (accessed August 13, 2014).

    Arlene G. Taylor (2006) provides the following definition: "Cataloging. The process of creating surrogate records for information packages by describing the information package, choosing name and title access points, conducting subject analysis, assigning subject headings and classification numbers, and maintaining the system through which the records are made available" (p. 528–529).

    In her online dictionary, Reitz (2004) defines cataloging as "the process of creating entries for a catalog. In libraries, this usually includes bibliographic description, subject analysis, assignment of classification notation, and activities involved in physically preparing the item for the shelf, tasks usually performed under the supervision of a librarian trained as a cataloger."

2. "[NISO Celebrates 70 Years]." 2009. *Information Standards Quarterly* http://www.niso.org/about/NISO_milestone_timeline_fromISQ.pdf

3. Charles Ammi Cutter. 1904. *Rules for a Dictionary Catalog*. Fourth edition, rewritten. Washington, D.C.: Government Printing Office. p. 12 http://digital.library.unt.edu/ark:/67531/metadc1048/ (accessed February 26, 2015).

4. IFLA Study Group on the Functional Requirements for Bibliographic Records. 2009. *Functional Requirements for Bibliographic Records: Final Report*. München: K.G.

Saur. http://www.ifla.org/files/assets/cataloguing/frbr/frbr_2008.pdf (accessed February 28, 2015)

5. Library of Congress Subject Headings. 2015, January. *Library of Congress.* (37th ed.) p. vii. http://www.loc.gov/aba/publications/FreeLCSH/lcshintro.pdf (accessed April 8, 2015).

6. IFLA Study Group. 2009.

7. Joint Steering Committee for Development of RDA: JSC Membership, 1974–. 2013. JSC-RDA. http://www.rda-jsc.org/jscmembers.html (accessed April 7, 2015).

8. Ibid.

CHAPTER 2

ILSs and the Online Library Catalog

In order for cataloging records to be searched and used, they need to be stored in specialized computer systems that can read the file types. Although cataloging records are electronic files, they are not actually web-ready. In an era of easily posting HTML documents to the web or creating blog posts through specialized blogging software online, library catalog records require a different approach: they must be manipulated using specialized software that is currently only used in libraries. This chapter describes these specialized library systems and gives a foundation for thinking about where and how the records catalogers create are ultimately stored for use by a variety of librarians and patron users.

The electronic cataloging records that catalogers create are housed in specialized databases called integrated library systems (ILSs). ILSs are different from standard databases in a few ways: first, they are meant to store, search, and display library data (i.e., MARC [Machine-Readable Cataloging] records), and they permit a variety of library-specific functions to be carried out. It makes sense that circulation work is going to require different interactions with the records in the ILS than acquisitions, cataloging, or work maintaining the technology such as in library systems offices. ILSs permit different groups to access records for library materials in a way that is appropriate to the tasks they need to carry out.

A number of ILSs exist, and due to mergers and buyouts, many commercial ILS vendors offer more than one ILS. Vendors include Ex Libris, Innovative Interfaces Incorporated (III), and Online Computer Library Center, Inc. (OCLC). Some ILSs, like Koha and Evergreen, are open-source, meaning that the underlying code is free to modify. Specialized vendors may host these open-source ILSs for libraries, or libraries can host the

Table 2.1 A Sample of Library Automation Companies and Selected ILSs[1]

Library Automation Companies	Integrated Library Systems (ILSs)
ByWater Solutions	Koha (hosting)
Ex Libris	Aleph 500; Voyager
Innovative Interfaces Inc.	Sierra; Millennium
OCLC	WorldShare Management Services
Polaris	Polaris
SirsiDynix	Unicorn; Horizon
VTLS	Virtua

ILS software on their own. Choosing an ILS is a complex decision and, as we will see next, may be one that is made as part of a group like a consortium. Table 2.1 shows a quick summary of companies and products that libraries may use.

NEXT-GEN SYSTEMS AND DISCOVERY SYSTEMS

The ILS is the system that library staff works with on the back end; the back end is the part of the system that houses the records. Interfaces allowing back-end access tend to be built for information professionals and allow them to carry out library-related tasks such as acquisitions and cataloging. All ILSs have built-in front ends, the interface that the patrons use to search for materials that librarians sometimes refer to as the online public access catalog (OPAC). Unfortunately, a lot of ILSs that have been around for a long time may have a somewhat user-unfriendly, patron-facing front end!

Next-generation (next-gen) front ends like ProQuest's AquaBrowser (http://www .proquest.com/products-services/AquaBrowser.html) and like BiblioCommons's Bib-lioCore (http://www.bibliocommons.com/products/bibliocore) allow patrons not only to search the content of the library's holdings but also to add comments or tags to records and to create and share lists with other users.

Academic or research libraries may opt to provide searchers access through a *discovery system.* Discovery systems are user-friendly, next-generation front ends that include the ability to search all of the library's content from a single search box. Although they do not tend to allow for comments or tagging, they are as intuitive as Google. In discovery systems, not only are patrons searching the library's catalog, they are also potentially searching the library's journal-article databases, vendor-supplied ebooks, their institutional repository contents, and even other online resources not held in the library such as the HathiTrust materials.

Discovery systems, also called discovery services, represent a new era in access for users. Discovery systems create a single index of all included content, making for a fast, efficient, and user-friendly experience, making discovery a certain future direction for library technology and catalogers to keep in mind. At present, many of the vendors offering ILSs also offer a discovery system. BiblioCommons's BiblioCore, mentioned earlier, is also a discovery system used primarily in public libraries; Ex Libris offers a product called Primo, ProQuest offers Summon, and OCLC offers WorldCat Discovery Services.

HISTORY: EVOLUTION OF NEXT-GENERATION CATALOGS

Online library catalogs began as simple digitized versions of the card catalog. Command-line searches were carried out in a clunky DOS environment. Searches in these systems were simple left-anchored character-string matches in a specific index. For example, "T:Of mice and" would return the title: Of mice and men. Typographical errors (on the part of either the patron or the cataloger) meant that results were not returned. These catalogs were electronic, but they were not available through the Internet.

The subsequent generation of library catalogs appeared in the 1990s after the web had begun to penetrate. Graphical user interfaces (GUIs) were more visually appealing but, for the most part, still offered the same limited searches as the previous generation. They were searchable through the web though, taking the catalog out of the library and into workplaces and homes.

Finally, next-generation catalogs began to appear in the 2000s. They included features that made them more similar to web-based tools, including *Did you mean* suggestions, visualizations of results, and social elements like tags. Since that time, full-blown front ends have been providing more web-friendly access to library catalog contents.

CATALOGING AND THE ILS

Catalogers interact with the ILS through the cataloging module. This module permits catalogers to create records or to import records that were created elsewhere and to modify those records based on local circumstances (e.g., indicating the call number the locally held item has, linking the bar code to the record, or making a note about a missing page in an item). Through the cataloging module, catalogers can indicate to the system where the item will be located (sometimes using a special MARC format, *MARC for Holdings*), and may be able to see order records, selector names, and costs of materials.

THE SHELF LIST

A library's shelf list, in the old days, was essentially a card catalog–based inventory of the library's holdings. It was primarily available for staff use and provided insight into the collection as a whole since it was organized according to call number. With automated systems, there no longer is a standalone shelf list that functions as an inventory of a collection's items. Through the cataloging module of the ILS, however, it is possible for catalogers to see where on a physical shelf an item will be placed after it has been processed. When catalogers talk about *shelflisting* today, they are concerned with making sure that the item they are cataloging will sit on the shelf in the correct place relative to the other items that are already there.

Of course, library staff members are not the only ones consulting the records in the ILS—the patrons are too! Patrons often will consult the ILS through a special web-based interface designed for non-staff use, the OPAC, or simply the *online library catalog*. Thirty years ago, patrons might have accessed catalog records through a divided card catalog, with separate sections for searching by authors, titles, and subjects. The *headings* at the top left-hand side of the card would have been used to place the card alphabetically in the drawers. In today's digitized environment, patrons are still able to search on these three kinds of terms in the online catalog. We call these the author (or creator) index, the title index, and the subject index. Depending on how content is encoded in the MARC record, it will appear as a result when these indexes are searched. For example, a series title will be indexed with the titles. That way, when a patron searches the title index for the *Ivy & Bean* series, all 10 of the *Ivy & Bean* series books will appear in the list of results if they are held by the library.

A number of the terms that can be searched in these indexes are controlled vocabulary terms. Controlled vocabularies standardize the way information is supplied in records, allowing for consistency in the catalog. Personal name access points and subject headings are examples of controlled vocabularies. Results of browses of a given index are alphabetized according to library-specific rules that govern the order in which these terms are returned. At first blush, it might seem as if alphabetizing results is a straightforward task, but given the complexity of last names and the various parts of speech of subject headings and their subheadings, providing a consistent display takes a fair bit of forethought.

In the days of card catalogs, it was only possible for patrons to search the catalog for authors (i.e., creators), titles, and subjects. In the current MARC environment, patrons can also do a keyword search. For example, if a book is a manga, a Japanese comic book with a bit of a cult following in the United States, the official subject heading assigned will be Comic books, strips, and so on. The word *manga* might not be included in the title, rendering the material very difficult to find using "manga" as a search term.

Keyword searching, however, allows the system to provide results in the list of hits that include terms not coming from the title, author, or subject fields. For example, if the library's system permits keyword searching of the summary field in the MARC record, and if the cataloger entered a summary that included the character string m-a-n-g-a, then the keyword search will put up this record for consideration.

When doing a keyword search, patrons are generally able to search the contents of the MARC records that have been provided by catalogers and that are included in the search. Commonly, these fields have content such as the International Standard Book Number (ISBN), tables of contents, summaries, and various other kinds of notes about the item. When keyword searches are carried out, the system must find a way to display the results in a coherent manner, based on relevance if possible.

Complex algorithms, not unlike those used by Google and other Internet search engines, govern the order in which the results are displayed, ideally with the most relevant hits appearing first. To understand how relevance works, it is necessary to think like a machine. If the keyword being searched is *dogs,* the library system will consider books relevant that have the character string d-o-g-s in the title, in the notes (e.g., table of contents) fields, or potentially in the subject heading field if the search term matches a subject heading. Of the items that are about *dogs,* the system will then consider the items identified and rank them so that those most about dogs are listed first since they will be the most relevant.

Local Practice

Because each institution is unique and each institution's users are unique, *local practice* develops in each institution. Catalogers carry out their craft adhering to the standards mentioned in Chapter 1, yet when there is cause for interpretation of the instructions, catalogers must formally establish the way they will proceed. This provides for consistency among the records in the local catalog. At times, it is difficult to separate out what is professional cataloging practice, what is local practice, and what is prescribed in the text of the standards themselves. In this book, we have decided to present the standards as they are practiced in the United States, with our own interpretations that provide for a maximum of access when in doubt. Your institution may have its own local practice that differs slightly from what is recommended here. Additionally, when given a choice, you may need to decide upon a practice and document your decision locally.

Local practice is a great thing: it allows for a degree of flexibility within a standards-based environment. Local practice, however, needs to be understood for what it is: it is one institution's take on providing consistent access. When in doubt, institutions should always opt to adopt practice that is used widely. Local practice should be documented and adhered to consistently; it should also be evaluated periodically and updated as needed. Catalogers need to understand where local practice begins and ends; this will keep them from supplying records created according to local practice into shared cataloging environments.

Beyond the Local Catalog

Local catalogs only include locally held material and can answer the question, "Does the library have x?" Union catalogs, instead, can help answer the question, "Does x exist?" Union catalogs are comprehensive collections of records for library materials. In the first half of the twentieth century, for example, a National Union Catalog (NUC) was published by the Library of Congress (LC) featuring small card catalog cards, in alphabetical order by author last name, for every book known to be published, by year. Libraries could create cards for their own collections based on the cards in the NUC, and researchers could confirm the existence of materials. Today, union catalogs are online and, in the case of the cataloging utility WorldCat (http://www.worldcat.org/) by OCLC, are composed of MARC records created in a distributed fashion by catalogers in different physical locations. Cataloging utilities are services that supply catalog records to individual institutions.

Some institutions have decided to work together and to consolidate cataloging work. In shared cataloging environments like consortia, for example, libraries can band together, sharing to some extent an ILS and records. In these cases, each library still has a local catalog through its own ILS, but there is also a shared catalog from which to take records. Shared catalogs tend to work best when libraries are similar in some respect. For example, academic libraries in a particular geographic location might choose to develop a shared catalog; school libraries in a district might develop a shared catalog, or rural public libraries in a particular county might develop a shared catalog. Benefits to consortial cataloging could include negotiating a better price for the ILS, having cataloging staff spend less time doing redundant work at multiple locations, and having a supportive network for troubleshooting issues and sharing best practices and approaches.

Decisions can be made to outsource some aspects of an institution's cataloging operations. As we saw, standards allow cataloging agencies to share catalog records. Buying records from the vendor at the same time that materials are purchased is one possibility. It is also possible to acquire records after materials have been acquired. Some ILSs come with Z39.50 capability (discussed further in Chapter 10). These systems allow staff to search for MARC records in freely available catalogs and to import them directly into the library's ILS. For example, a record for a recent best-seller might exist in LC's database; if so, it can be extracted using the Z39.50 protocol. Academic and larger public libraries may be paying members of OCLC. As members, they search in and download records from the cataloging module of OCLC's WorldCat.

Outsourcing certain workflows or aspects of processing is also possible. Cataloging of a certain kind of materials such as audiovisual items or foreign-language materials can be outsourced or done by special arrangement through contract hiring. Additionally, purchasing items from library vendors that are shelf-ready (barcoded, labeled with the call number, etc.) is a kind of outsourcing that will permit catalogers to spend more time doing the intellectual work of cataloging.

CONCLUSION

Library cataloging depends a great deal on the systems that house and make available the records. These ILSs are built with current library standards in mind, permitting records to be stored and retrieved in a systematic way. Not every library needs to catalog every book, but good cataloging is no less important simply because some records can be shared. Every library owes it to its patrons to have the best catalog it can, making items as accessible to all as possible.

NOTE

1. Table based on: Breeding, Marshall. 2014. *Library Technology Guides*. http://library technology.org/ (accessed August 14, 2014).

CHAPTER 3

Materials and Approaches in Library Cataloging

⟩

Libraries collect many different types of materials—much more than just books. In general, the cataloging rules apply to all formats, but each type of item has unique aspects that have to be considered. In this chapter, we describe some of the different kinds of materials that libraries might collect, and give some perspective on how they are handled when it comes to cataloging with RDA.

It comes down to the fact that the way catalogers describe and provide access to objects that are meant to be read by human beings will differ from the way they describe and provide access to objects that are meant to be read by computers or other devices. . . . Standard print books do not require anything additional beyond one's eyes, but DVDs require a computer with specific hardware and software. Good cataloging records will reflect these and other differences in format that will have an impact on the use and usability of materials by patrons since, when it comes down to it, the book *Gone with the Wind* is not exactly the same thing as the DVD by the same name.

CONTENT, MEDIA, AND CARRIER TYPE

RDA helps catalogers and library users separate the *content,* the creative or scholarly "meat," from the *carrier,* or the way that meat is presented. RDA also is concerned about the media, the kinds of devices or software needed to access the content on a certain carrier. In the days of AACR2, this kind of information was only consistently provided for non-print materials, and even then, it was included very awkwardly with the title, seriously hindering search!

Today, cataloging records in RDA include formal information about the Content Type (RDA 6.9), Media Type (RDA 3.2), and Carrier Type (RDA 3.3) for all items being cataloged—this not only helps with retrieval of non-print items but also better reflects the growing complexity of the materials in library collections. Each is examined more closely next.

Content Type

Content Type is a *core element* in RDA, meaning that RDA requires information about Content Type to be included in all cataloging records. According to RDA, Content Type "is a categorization reflecting the fundamental form of communication in which the content is expressed and the human sense through which it is intended to be perceived."[1] Essentially, Content Type is linked to the way the material is presented: is this a written text, performed music, or something else? RDA provides a controlled vocabulary, or a list, of terms that can be used to fill in the Content Type information in RDA 6.9.1.3 Recording Content Type (RDA Table 6.1). In this *Crash Course,* we will focus primarily on cataloging traditional print books and are most interested in *text*: "Content expressed through a form of notation for language intended to be perceived visually."[2]

Things start to get a little complex, however, when comparing traditional print monographs, e-books, and audiobooks. Traditional print books and e-books are both *text* resources; audiobooks on compact discs or on Playaways are sound recordings, specifically of the *spoken word*.

Media Type

According to RDA, Media Type "is a categorization reflecting the general type of intermediation device required to view, play, run, etc., the content of a resource."[3] The idea behind Media Type is to be general in identifying the kinds of resources needed for consuming the content. Table 3.1 in RDA 3.2.1.3 Recording Media Type is used to supply Media Type terms for the various formats that libraries collect. Conveniently enough, the Media Types relate directly to the Carrier Types. They are: audio, computer, microform, projected image, stereographic, unmediated, and video.

For traditional print monographs, the Media Type is *unmediated. Unmediated* is probably the most interesting for discussion in this *Crash Course,* because unmediated means that only the users' eyes, and no additional devices, are necessary to "view" the content.

Carrier Type

Tightly tied to the idea of Media Type is the idea of Carrier Type. Carrier Type, a core element in RDA, "is a categorization reflecting the format of the storage medium and housing of a carrier in combination with the type of intermediation device required to view, play, run, etc., the content of a resource."[4] In short, Carrier Type is another way of naming the format; it is a more specific way of naming a Media Type, and a resource may have more than one Carrier Type, just as it may have more than one Media Type. A list of Carrier Types is given in RDA 3.3.1.3 Recording Carrier Type for the categories described earlier: audio, computer, microform, projected image, stereographic, unmediated, and video. For example, audio carriers include audiocassette, audiotape reel, and sound-track reel; computer carriers include computer disc and online resource, and unmediated carriers include card, flipchart, object, sheet, and volume. Traditional print books are, in terms of the Carrier Types listed, a *volume*.

It may be fair to say that much of this seems completely obvious, especially when it comes to traditional books. As the formats held in libraries become increasingly diverse, however, it is a good thing to have a record of the kinds of formats held and the kinds of devices required in order to consume that content.

In the remainder of this chapter, the different kinds of materials that might be found in a library are described, along with their Content Type, Media Type, and Carrier Type. The formats collected will vary from library to library. Although this *Crash Course* focuses on cataloging traditional print books, other common materials and their interesting attributes are described here in a cursory way. This should provide a bit of context for thinking about the different kinds of materials that might end up in a given library—and how those formats will be described in the library catalog.

MONOGRAPHS (AKA BOOKS)

Traditional print books still make up the largest percentage of most library collections and are the main focus of this guide, so this is a reasonable place to begin a discussion of library materials and formats. Although it is easy to talk about "traditional print books," FRBR is careful not to use the colloquial term "books" since there are too many potential meanings.[5] RDA, in keeping with FRBR and with the cataloging tradition, follows the AACR2 practice of referring to books (the format) as "monographs." The RDA glossary defines a monograph as "a resource that is complete in one part or intended to be completed within a finite number of parts."[6]

For the remainder of this section, then, the more precise term *monographs* will be used instead. The Content Type for print monographs is *text,* the Media Type is *unmediated,* and the Carrier Type is *volume.*

Monographs themselves are quite complex, owing in part to the rich history of printing and bookbinding. Sidebar 3.1 is a Terminology Alert identifying different parts of traditional print monographs. As with other aspects of professional cataloging, there is a certain amount of jargon used by catalogers in describing monographs. Although best practices indicate that libraries should never use professional jargon in patron-facing parts of the online library catalog, anyone doing cataloging will need to understand some basic terms that appear quite regularly in descriptive cataloging using RDA.

SIDEBAR 3.1   TERMINOLOGY ALERT: PARTS OF A MONOGRAPH (I.E., A BOOK)

Title page: The formal stating of the title and creators of the book. Often includes the publisher and the place of publication.

Title page verso: The back side of the title page. This page usually includes expanded publisher information and copyright information. If the book has Cataloging in Publication (CIP) data (this often looks like a mini card catalog card that is missing information about things like the number of pages and size), it will be located here.

Colophon: Includes the same information as the title page verso, but it is found at the back of the book. Common in picture books, artistic photography books, and books produced in France.

Preliminary pages: Pages that are usually numbered using lowercase Roman numerals, found toward the beginning of a book, where information like the table of contents, tables of illustrations, and even the foreword or the preface are given.

Pages: Sheets of paper that are printed on both sides (or that *can* be printed on both sides) bound together.

Illustrations: Images of any kind; in other words, content that cannot be created using a keyboard. Illustrations include things like images (including re-printings of physical photographs), maps, and portraits. RDA tells us all of these are "illustrations." In the old days, illustrations were by default black and white. We record information about color illustrations in cataloging records.

Cover: The outside of the book, consisting of front cover, back cover, and spine.

Bibliographical references: Works that are referenced by the author. These may be found in footnotes, at the end of each chapter, or in one list at the end of the book.

Filmography: A list of movies and television shows, generally, that an actor, producer, director, and others have been involved in.

Webliography: A list of web resources either cited in a book or suggested for further information.

RDA provides instructions to allow catalogers to carry out descriptive cataloging. RDA allows catalogers to create the parts of the cataloging record focusing on the physical characteristics and their related access points. Beyond these physical characteristics and related access points, two primary sets of characteristics not related to the item's physical traits will affect how traditional print monographs are cataloged: one has to do with the *content* of the item and the other, with its intended audience. These categories break down as fiction versus nonfiction and juvenile versus adult. Each set is presented and discussed next.

Fiction versus Nonfiction Monographs

There is more to cataloging than just describing an item's physical characteristics; there is also what it is *about*. Descriptive cataloging and the creation of access points according to RDA are identical for fiction and for nonfiction, but treatment beyond that will differ slightly for the two.

When cataloging fiction, the trickiest aspect will likely be creating subject headings. Sometimes this is because it can be hard to figure out exactly what the item is about. At other times, it is because it can be necessary to separate aboutness (subject headings) from what an item is (genre heading). These will be discussed in more detail in Chapter 8. In literature classes in universities around the world, the true meaning of great literary works continues to be debated. For example, what is *Hamlet* truly about, on the deepest levels? How then can cataloging librarians possibly identify the true aboutness of these works for patrons? Yet, in an effort to provide access, an attempt should be made to include subject headings if at all possible. Academic libraries in the past have left them off, especially in adult general fiction, but this is changing.

In recent years, a push has been made to separate genre headings (what an item *is* in terms of its form, e.g., Horror films) from subject headings (what an item is *about*, e.g., Haunted houses). Separating them in cataloging allows online public-access catalogs (OPACs) to differentiate between the two types of headings for searching purposes. Genre headings can also be used to help classify items if the fiction collection is separated (general, fantasy, Christian, etc.).

For most of cataloging history, summaries were rarely included in cataloging records for adult fiction. However, in recent years, the ability to copy and paste summaries from websites has allowed for an increase in the number of summaries. These summaries are still not required, and the cataloger may decide not to add them, but they do no harm and should be left if present in cataloging copy (for a reminder about the difference between original cataloging and copy cataloging, see Chapter 1).

Nonfiction titles can be a bit more problematic. In addition to needing good subject analysis and classification (see Chapters 8 and 9), there are other aspects of the book that need to be taken into consideration. Should the table of contents be transcribed? The additional terms in essence add keywords to a record and can assist with retrieval in keyword searches. Is a bibliography or index present (aids researchers in deciding if a book is appropriate or not)? The Library of Congress (LC) considers bibliographies and indexes to be core and will include information about them in their cataloging records. Is there special information in a glossary or appendix that needs to be mentioned? LC will not consistently add that information, but catalogers may decide to establish a local policy to include it.

Juvenile versus Adult Monographs

In talking about cataloging, the default tends to be a discussion of items intended for adults. Items intended for juveniles can have additional considerations, in part because juvenile users of library catalogs are not likely to be as sophisticated as adult users, but also because the materials are just different.

For example, sometimes it can be hard to tell if a picture book is fiction or nonfiction. When this happens, there is not one right answer. Catalogers should classify it where they think it would be best for their users. Another question is the age group (easy, juvenile, YA [young adult]) where an item should be classed. As a rule, catalogers will not infer information that they cannot find on the book. For example, most board books/picture books go in easy, but a picture book with a lot of text or on a weightier topic may need to go in a different section. Depending on the collection and the use and users, some libraries may opt to put stickers on the spines of juvenile items linked to particular holidays (e.g., Halloween) or on particular topics (e.g., diversity), so this may be an additional consideration for catalogers. Finally, LC policy requires that books intended for children include a summary, although summaries are often left off nonfiction titles if there is a good table of contents.

CONTINUING RESOURCES

Continuing resources is, like *monographs,* a technical term used in the Anglo-American Cataloguing Rules, Second Edition (AACR2) to help describe particular types of materials found in libraries. As the name might imply, continuing resources are items that do not have a definite end. Although the term continuing resource is not used in RDA, it represents a useful notion; we identify two types of continuing resources in RDA: serials and integrating resources. In terms of cataloging, each will have its own Content Type (probably *text*); it will also have Media Types and Carrier Types depending on the format (e.g., unmediated, volume; computer, online resource).

Serials

Serials are, according to RDA, items "issued in successive parts" and do not have a predetermined end.[7] Common types of serials include newspapers, magazines, journals, and newsletters. The main thing to remember when cataloging serials is that the record needs to be very broad and general, because it refers to the entire run, not just a single issue or two. Because of the changeable nature of serials, they are often quite challenging to catalog, and the work is specialized within the cataloging community. Unlike monograph records, serial records often require updating after they have been downloaded to the catalog. When working with serials there are a number of things to watch for, including the following:

- Has the title changed? If so, is it a minor title change, needing just an update to the record, or is it a major change requiring a new record?
- Has the frequency and/or numbering changed?
- Are there any numbering discrepancies?
- Are there special issues/supplements that need to be accounted for?
- Is a title still active or has it ceased publication?

Because of a lack of time and resources, many libraries do not make non-critical updates, such as frequency changes, to serial cataloging records. However, attempts should be made to keep up with critical changes, like title changes.

Another question that arises with serials is "how many records?" Libraries often have holdings for one title in multiple formats (print, microform, online). The Program for Cooperative Cataloging (PCC) sponsors the Cooperative Online Serials Program (CONSER) to assist catalogers with this. CONSER requires that each different format receives its own record. However, most non-CONSER libraries ignore this rule and put all of their holdings on one record. This is generally considered more user-friendly, as patrons only have to look at one record to know if the library holds the specific issue needed.

Integrating Resources

According to RDA, integrating resources are items that have different parts of them updated at different times.[8] All websites are considered integrating resources since it is common to update the contents of a single page or to add a page to the website. In the late

1990s and early 2000s, many libraries were excited by the idea of being able to catalog websites. However, enthusiasm waned when the sheer volume of websites became clear; not only that, the idea of keeping the records up-to-date with the current version of the website seemed just about impossible.

In print form, most integrating resources are kept in binders. At certain intervals, replacement pages will be issued by the publisher. Someone will then need to remove the superseded pages and insert the new ones. The print version of RDA and its predecessor AACR2 are examples of integrating resources. Identifying the date correctly is frequently the trickiest part about cataloging integrating resources.

AUDIOVISUAL MATERIALS

RDA does not define *audiovisual (A/V) materials,* but instead treats each non-text, mediated format separately. In libraries, though, catalogers tend to refer to A/V materials collectively as the expressions that are not print-based and not readable with just the human eye. Practically speaking, the variety of formats that A/V materials represent can be a challenge to description and access in libraries. Next, we describe videos, audiobooks, and musical sound recordings. Each will have its own Content Type, Carrier Type, and Media Type that will also be mentioned below.

DVDs/Blu-rays

DVDs and other video recordings are much more complicated to catalog than monographs. First and foremost, more people are involved in the production of the content that is viewed through the DVD (there are potentially writers, producers, directors, cast members, film editors, lighting crews, and others). In addition, there are many more notes that should be added to the cataloging record since people cannot flip through a DVD like they do a book. Examples include things like special features, subtitles, deleted scenes, making of, and crew members. In terms of the Content, the Media, and the Carrier Types, DVDs are two-dimensional moving image (Content Type), video (Media Type), and videodisc (Carrier Type).

Original cataloging of DVDs should be done from the viewed item, not the surface of the disc or the case. Ideally, copy cataloging should also be done this way, although it is not always feasible. Regardless, the DVD should be tested to make sure that it is the correct item, that menu items work, and that the program/movie plays. Although technical problems are rare, they do occur from time to time and are easier to take care of before the item is checked out to a patron. Some additional things to watch out for or note:

- If you have a Blu-ray or something other than a standard DVD, make sure that the record reflects this as prominently as possible. If a disc will not play in all players or special equipment is needed, this should also be mentioned.
- Widescreen or full screen should be noted if known.
- Foreign language features/subtitles should be noted.
- Captioning, audio description, and sign language should be noted. These are especially important as they may be needed to show evidence of items with accessibility.

- Cast notes for television shows and feature films should be added if possible. Patrons will search for favorite actors. The main actors should also be given access points (discussed in Chapter 7).
- As with actors, producers, directors, and writers should also be noted.
- If the item is based on a book or another piece of literature, this should be noted, along with an access point for the work (also discussed in Chapter 7).
- Summaries should be included.

The Online Audiovisual Catalogers, Inc. (OLAC) is an international organization for the cataloging of non-print materials. They offer workshops on a variety of topics for both beginner and advanced catalogers. Their website, http://www.olacinc.org, offers practical information and best practices.

Spoken Word Sound Recordings

Most spoken sound recordings will be audiobooks, but they also include radio plays and recorded speeches and interviews. Audiobooks will be cataloged just like the print versions, but with added information about the audio format, including information about the reader(s) and running time. Summaries are often added to the cataloging record as well. If an item is abridged, this should be noted.

In terms of the Content, the Media, and the Carrier Types, spoken word recordings on CD are spoken word (Content Type), audio (Media Type), and audio disc (Carrier Type). If the recording is available on a Playaway, then the Carrier Type is *other*.

Music Sound Recordings

Music sound recordings can be divided into two categories: classical and non-classical. Classical CDs are the harder of the two because of the access points. Luckily for non-specialists, good copy, meaning existing cataloging records for the materials, is frequently available. Access points for musical works may be extremely complex—they often begin with the name of the composer and are followed by a long string of detailed information about the way the music is performed; this can include the instruments used, the key in which the music was played, and possibly whether the music was changed from the original composition. At first blush, this might look more complicated than what patrons need, but access points for musical works should be included in the record if at all possible.

Additionally, some notes are expected to help patrons better understand what is included on the disc. All music CDs should include a contents note providing detailed information about the titles of the songs. If the running time is noted on the disc, it should be added to the cataloging record. Total running time for the entire disc, as well as individual running times for specific songs, should be included. Music CDs will have an RDA Content Type of performed music, a Media Type of audio, and a Carrier Type of audio disc.

EBOOKS

Practical aspects of ebooks cataloging depend on whether the ebooks are bought individually or as a subscription. Subscriptions of ebooks are often bundled in the hundreds, if not thousands, making it nearly impossible for an individual library to catalog them all. In the case of subscriptions, most libraries also purchase the accompanying MARC records from the vendors from whom they acquire the ebooks. These cataloging records are generally of good quality, although a sample should be checked for accuracy and to decide if any local changes need to be made.

If only a few ebook titles are being purchased, they are usually cataloged by the library. They are cataloged just like a print book, with a few modifications to indicate that the book is digital, rather than print. If fact, most ebook records are derived from the print version record.

In terms of the Content, the Media, and the Carrier Types, ebooks are text (Content Type), computer (Media Type), and online resource (Carrier Type).

GOVERNMENT DOCUMENTS

In most respects, the cataloging of government documents does not differ from other cataloging. What is different is the classification system. Dewey Decimal Classification (DDC) and Library of Congress Classification (LCC) both arrange their systems by topic/subject. The federal government documents scheme, SuDocs, is based on the entity publishing the document. After receiving the designation for the publishing agency, government documents are numbered in the order they were produced, and then given a Cutter number (i.e., an author number) based on the title of the document. Most states have their own similar classification scheme for state government documents.

LOCAL ITEMS

Libraries will invariably collect items of local interest, both physical and electronic. The publishing quality of these will vary significantly. Catalogers should catalog them as best as they can. Librarians may also want to consider having a special physical location for these types of items and even a special access point in the catalog to distinguish them from other materials.

CONCLUSION

It might be tempting to think that items should be hurried through the cataloging process as quickly as possible so that they can be put out on the shelves and used. Although processing items in a timely manner is a worthy goal, taking a little bit of extra time on the cataloging can significantly increase the likelihood of items being found in the catalog. Understanding some of the intricacies of the different formats goes a long way in helping ensure that will happen.

NOTES

1. Content Type. Glossary. *RDA Toolkit*. http://access.rdatoolkit.org/
2. Text. Glossary. *RDA Toolkit*. http://access.rdatoolkit.org/

3. Media Type. Glossary. *RDA Toolkit*. http://access.rdatoolkit.org/
4. Carrier Type. Glossary. *RDA Toolkit*. http://access.rdatoolkit.org/
5. Barbara Tillett. 2003. *What Is FRBR?: A Conceptual Model for the Bibliographic Universe*. Library of Congress Cataloging Distribution Service. http://loc.gov/cds/downloads/FRBR.PDF (accessed April 8, 2015)
6. Monograph. Glossary. *RDA Toolkit*. http://access.rdatoolkit.org/
7. Serial. Glossary. *RDA Toolkit*. http://access.rdatoolkit.org/
8. The RDA Toolkit glossary defines Integrating Resource as "a resource that is added to or changed by means of updates that do not remain discrete but are integrated into the whole (e.g., a loose-leaf manual that is updated by means of replacement pages, a website that is updated continuously)."

SUGGESTED RESOURCES

Serials Cataloging

CONSER Cataloging Manual. Available in Cataloger's Desktop. See http://www.loc.gov/cds/desktop/.

Training materials for the Basic Serials Cataloging Workshop. (2014 revision). http://www.loc.gov/aba/pcc/conser/scctp/basicppt.html

A/V Materials Cataloging

Online Audiovisual Catalogers, Inc. (OLAC) http://www.olacinc.org is an international organization for the cataloging of non-print materials. They offer workshops on a variety of topics for both beginner and advanced catalogers. Their website offers practical information and best practices.

Sound Recordings Cataloging

The Music Cataloging at Yale website (http://www.library.yale.edu/cataloging/music/musicat.htm) originally began as an internal site for the use of their own catalogers, but today it is considered an authoritative website for music cataloging information.

The Music Library Association (MLA) is concerned with all areas of music librarianship, including cataloging. They have written a best practices document for music cataloging, http://www.musiclibraryassoc.org/resource/resmgr/BCC_RDA/RDA_Best_Practices_v1.0.pdf.

CHAPTER 4

Encoding RDA Cataloging Records

In many ways, library cataloging is about standards being applied—standards for description, for subject access, and also for sharing and presenting that data. Card catalog cards adhered to standards in terms of size (3 x 5"), and there were conventions about how data appeared on them (headings and call numbers, etc.). Today, catalogers use MAchine-Readable Cataloging (MARC; pronounced *mark*), a special encoding standard used only in libraries, to share and present cataloging data electronically.

In this chapter, we explain just enough about MARC to make you dangerous. We start by situating MARC and providing some background. We look at some MARC records, too. Then, we go through and describe three views of MARC bibliographic records: what the computer reads, what the cataloger sees, and what the patron sees. Along the way, we describe the technical elements required by catalogers to build a MARC record. Finally, we talk about other schema being used and we present some information on the schema that may one day replace MARC.

MARC AS AN ENCODING STANDARD

The encoding standard that libraries are currently using is MARC. MARC encodes the information held in catalog records. Once the catalog record is encoded, it can be stored, searched, and ultimately used. Library systems currently rely on MARC, and it is a big deal in sharing the catalog records libraries create.

To put it in perspective, MARC has been around since the 1960s. HTML, the common web markup language, has been around only since 1993. MARC not only encodes content about the resource but also provides information about the MARC record itself. In this way, it is not completely dissimilar from HTML! Except, as mentioned, MARC is only for library data, and it does not display directly on the web the way HTML does.

MARC was invented by a woman named Henriette Avram. Although Avram was not a librarian, she worked for the Library of Congress (LC) and had the foresight and vision to create an encoding scheme that would help libraries save both time and energy well into the future. After going through various iterations as described in Chapter 1, the MARC format in use now in the United States is MARC 21. MARC 21 is not version 21.0 of the MARC format. Instead, MARC 21 came from merging the MARC format used in the United States (US MARC) with the MARC format used in Canada (CANMARC) in the 1990s as MARC for the 21st century. MARC 21 also includes elements introduced in the 1990s through "format integration," where the MARC used to describe, for example, audiovisual (A/V) content, was also permitted to be used to describe text-based content like books.

The Library of Congress currently maintains the MARC 21 standard with input from various constituencies such as the American Library Association (ALA)'s Association for Library Collections and Technical Services/Library and Information Technology Association (ALCTS/LITA) Metadata Standards Committee (www.ala.org/lita/about/committees/Jnt-meta), formerly the Machine-Readable Bibliographic Information Committee (MARBI). Information about using MARC can be found on the LC website (http://www.loc.gov/marc/).

The Online Computer Library Center, Inc. (OCLC) is a nonprofit, member-driven bibliographic network that also supports the use of MARC in libraries. OCLC's *Bibliographic Formats and Standards* (http://oclc.org/bibformats/en.html) provides not only information about the use of MARC but also examples for OCLC member libraries to follow. This web resource is free, searchable through the use of its own search engine, and available for use to anyone wanting to learn more about specifics of applying MARC.

MARC is independent of RDA and even of AACR2, but in order to put MARC to work, *some* content standard needs to be selected. That way, the cataloger knows what content needs to be marked up and how that content should be presented. The examples in this chapter and in the appendix (Appendix A) show RDA records encoded in MARC.

MARC records have to encode library data but they also have to be read by the library's integrated library system (ILS). There are parts to the MARC record that catalogers see when cataloging, and parts that they do not see. MARC records ultimately allow patrons to view information about library content through the web interface, so they also have to be displayed properly through the graphical user interface (GUI) to the system. Patrons also do not see all of the MARC record, they just see enough to (1) find, (2) identify, (3) select, and (4) obtain the material!

THE STRUCTURE OF MARC RECORDS: WHAT THE CATALOGER DOESN'T SEE

Given their history and original purpose, it makes sense that MARC records were never meant to be seen by people. After all, they are *machine*-readable and not *human*-readable. The MARC 21 communications format allows for machines to exchange MARC records in a way that is machine-friendly. The communications format is not, however, terribly human-friendly. The cataloger does not see the communications format.

Why? Documentation dating back to 1996 explains that these records "do not mandate internal storage or display formats to be used by individual systems."[1] This means that raw MARC records, in the most basic, communications format, do not have *any* feature that makes them easily read by humans!

Catalogers do not see MARC records in this format. The systems librarian, however, may, and every once in a while, the cataloger may be asked to help out. In the communications format, the MARC record is a long string of numbers, letters, and spaces: characters typed with a standard keyboard. An example of the MARC communications format is given in Sidebar 4.1. The following record is for a book called *Gatsby: The Cultural History of the Great American Novel* written by Bob Batchelor. As you can see, it is very unreadable at first blush.

SIDEBAR 4.1   MARC 21 BIBLIOGRAPHIC RECORD (IN COMMUNICATIONS FORMAT) AND EXPLANATION

    ↓   ↓   ↓   ↓   ↓

```
01194cam a2200301 i 450000100090000000050017000009008004100026906004500067
92500490011295501540016101000170031502000390033202000260037104000280039704
20008004250500026004330820016004591000020004752450081004952640044005763000
02900620336002100649337002500673380023006954900037007185040067007556000070
00822-17808624-20140923152432.0-130711s2014 mdu b 001 0
eng-a7bcbccorignewd1eecipf20gy-gencatlg-0 aacquireb2 shelf copiesxSel/rj
c,2014-09-23-bxk14 2013-07-11ixk14 2013-07-11wxl47 2013-07-11 to CIPaxn08
2014-01-29 1 copy rec'd., to CIP ver.frm11 2014-04-25 CipVererm11 2014-04-
25 to CALM- a 2013024293- a9780810891951 (cloth : alk. paper)- z9780810891968
(ebook)- aDLCbengcDLCerdadDLC- apcc-00aPS3511.I9bG8228 2014-00a813/.522
23-1aBatchelor, Bob.-10aGatsby:bthe cultural history of the great American nov
el/cBobBatchelor.-1aLanham:bRowman & Littlefield,c[2014]-axvi, 299 pages;c
24cm.-atext2rdacontent-aunmediated2rdamedia-avolume2rdacarrier-0aConte
mporary American Literature- aIncludes bibliographical references (pages
287-294) and index.-10aFitzgerald, F. Scottq(Francis Scott),d1896-1940.t
Great Gatsby.-
```

And yet we are asking you to look at this record anyway. Based on your work with library catalogs, you will likely recognize some parts if you stare hard enough. The rest are easily explained.

The Leader

The integrated library system (ILS) understands that the first 24 characters in a MARC communications format record compose what is called the *leader*, i.e., the 24 characters up to the first little arrow in Sidebar 4.1. The leader is highly encoded information about the record that follows. It includes information about important aspects of the record so that it stores and displays it correctly. Information in the leader includes the character encoding scheme used (important for display) and information about the *flavor* of MARC (e.g., MARC 21 bibliographic, MARC 21 authority, or MARC 21 for holdings). Within MARC 21 bibliographic, there are MARC records for several kinds of formats, including

Books (BK), Continuing resources (CR) (previously Serials [SE]), Computer files (CF), Maps (MP), Music (MU), and Visual materials (VM).

No cataloger will see the record this way under normal circumstances, but will have to create at least some of the metadata that is included in the record's leader.

The Directory

After the leader in the MARC communications format comes the *directory*. The length of the directory is different from record to record, and is based on the actual *contents* of the record that will follow. The directory shows where content is in the record and describes using codes what that content is. It would be nearly impossible for a human to create a directory like this, but through the use of the system, it is easy to save the record that the cataloger sees (further discussion about the cataloger's view follows). That record is saved in the MARC communications format that the computer understands, stores, and can easily transmit. In Sidebar 4.1, the directory is the 23 sets of 12 digits following the leader. This is because the record has 23 lines of content (not including the leader). In Sidebar 4.1, each set of 12 digits in the first line of the directory is set off by little arrows.

The Contents

After the directory in the MARC communications format comes the actual content of the record itself. One of the fields included in this content area is the 008, a highly encoded field that provides specific information about the content in a way that in many cases allows the system to limit based on this content. Examples of information included in this highly encoded 008 field are dates of publication, audience level, and language.

Other parts of the record itself include codes, such as the ISBN. Additional content in the record includes information like the title, the author, and often the subject of the material. It is in this third chunk of information that data about the title, Gatsby: the cultural history of the great American novel; the author, Bob Batchelor; the publisher, Rowman & Littlefield; and the inferred date of publication, 2014, are found. Other expected information such as the pagination, 299 pages; the dimensions, 24 cm; this series, American Literature; notes, bibliographical references (pages 287–294) and index; and finally the subject heading, Fitzgerald, F. Scott (Francis Scott),1896–1940. *Great Gatsby* are also listed here.

THE STRUCTURE OF MARC RECORDS: WHAT THE CATALOGER SEES

Fortunately, catalogers do not have to look at the raw MARC communications format with its long string of illegible characters at the beginning. Each ILS that a librarian uses provides a slightly different interface for looking at and editing the MARC communications format records. It may not exactly be as human-readable as a newspaper page or as a word processing document, but the cataloger's view of the record is a vast improvement in terms of human readability over the computer-readable format in which it is stored.

As mentioned, each ILS is different. Some elements, however, will be identical from system to system. Aspects like help with encoding the highly encoded areas of the record such as the leader and the 008 are available in ILSs across the board, although that help might display differently to the cataloger from system to system. Additionally, in each ILS, there is the need for the cataloger to input information about the item based on the content standard being used.

Highly encoded content is added by the cataloger into the highly encoded areas of the record. In bibliographic utilities (e.g., OCLC and SkyRiver) the term *fixed fields* is used to describe some combination of the 008 MARC field and some content stored in the leader and potentially in the 007.[2] Because highly encoded content is difficult for humans to read, the fixed fields display the data in a more human-readable form. ILSs may or may not use fixed fields, or may call them by a different name. However, the point is same: it is necessary to make computer-readable information human-readable if catalogers are to enter information!

In practice, some of this highly encoded information is the content the computer uses when limiting searches based on refinements like date of publication, language, or audience.

In the cataloger's view, the fixed fields area gives visual prompts to the cataloger for filling in the highly encoded content. See Figure 4.1 for the fixed fields that OCLC chooses to display to catalogers in Connexion, the cataloger's module for accessing WorldCat.

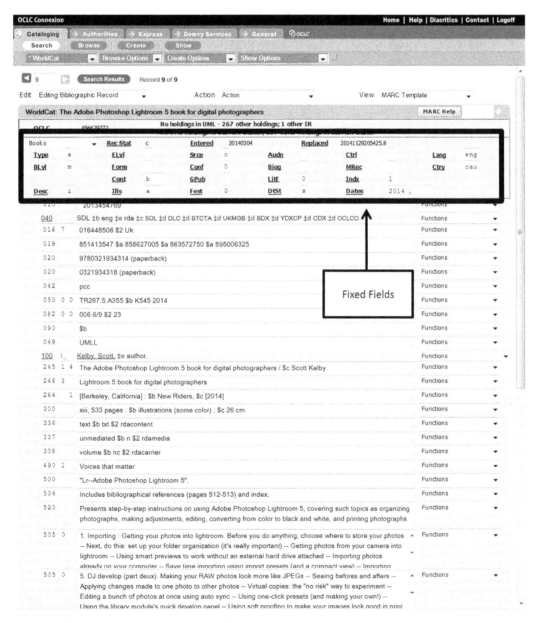

Figure 4.1   A Bibliographic Record in OCLC Connexion (Web Interface): Fixed Fields.

Fixed fields or highly encoded parts of the record can be contrasted with the variable fields. Variable fields are variable because they are not required and because the amount of information entered into them will vary from record to record. The variable fields area of the record includes information that can be encoded but also that can be free text. The ISBN is one example of a data field that is encoded in the MARC record (i.e., "variable control fields"), and the title is an example of free text in the MARC record (i.e., information encoded in a "variable data field").[3]

Anatomy of Variable Fields

When viewed using the cataloging module of the ILS or an online product like OCLC Connexion's web browser, the variable fields of the MARC record all follow the same pattern.

MARC Field Tags (MARC Tags)

The variable fields begin with a three-digit code, the *MARC field tag*, that describes to the computer the kind of information that follows. Is the rest of the content a title? A subject heading? An ISBN? A summary? There are many field tags that can be used, but there is a relatively small set that are used over and over. You will get to know the common MARC field tags the more you work with cataloging records. Next, you will find an illustration of the various parts of the variable field in MARC (see Figure 4.2). In this illustration and throughout this book, we put spaces both before and after the subfield delimiters for ease of reading. By now, you might have guessed that different ILSs may deal with spacing differently.

These three-digit MARC field codes are similar to HTML tags that describe the nature of the content being marked up (paragraph, heading, etc.). HTML tags tend to be words or letters based on a mnemonic. Most ILSs just use these three-digit codes. Koha is one example of an ILS that permits but does not require catalogers to use MARC tags when creating variable fields; the correct field tag is stored in the system nonetheless when the record is saved in the MARC communications format.

Indicators

After the MARC field tag, or *MARC tag*, two indicators appear, the first indicator and the second indicator. These tend to govern how the computer handles the content that follows. These indicators might explain how to index the content or whether to display it

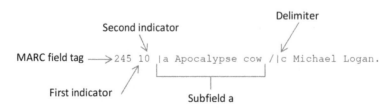

Figure 4.2   Anatomy of MARC Variable Fields.

to the patrons (versus only including it in when patrons carry out keyword searches). The two indicators might look like a single two-digit number, but they are two separate numbers, each with separate meaning. When looking up information about how a field should be used, there will also be instructions on how to encode the indicators. Sometimes they are left blank; sometimes only the first one is encoded, sometimes only the second, and sometimes both are encoded. It all depends on the MARC field tag and the content being encoded. Indicators primarily make it clear to the computer how content should be interpreted so that it can be searched and displayed. See Figure 4.3 for an example record in OCLC Connexion highlighting the use of indicators.

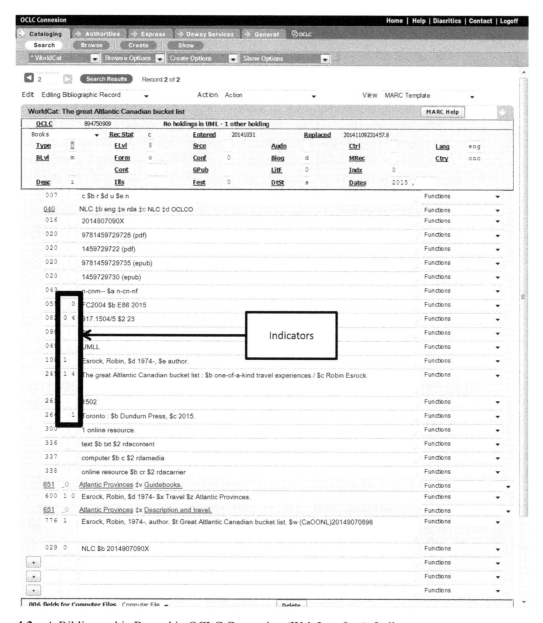

Figure 4.3 A Bibliographic Record in OCLC Connexion (Web Interface): Indicators.

An example of content that is not displayed to patrons but that is helpful to catalogers and that facilitates search in the system is *variant titles*. As Chapter 6 explains, catalogers always record the title of a book directly from the title page. Sometimes publishers include titles that are similar but not entirely identical on the spine or even on the cover. Although this additional information about titles is useful to a cataloger and could potentially assist a title searched by a patron, variant (additional) titles are included in the MARC record but if similar to the official, recorded title do not "print." This means that variant titles are not displayed to patrons through the web interface. How can content be included in the MARC record that is not shown to patrons? Indicators provide the necessary information to the system and help make sure that only essential content is displayed to users.

Subfields and Their Delimiters

The actual content of the field follows the indicators. The content is broken up into *subfields,* or smaller fields within the larger MARC fields. Subfields are generally named for letters of the alphabet, always given in lowercase, or, in some circumstances, numbers. Letters and numbers, however, look to a computer a lot like the content being encoded. In order for the system to understand where one subfield begins and another ends, there has to be some systematic way to distinguish how the two are separated. Delimiters are the answer!

Although the term *delimiters* sounds vaguely like one of Harry Potter's nemeses, in MARC records, delimiters just separate subfields within the MARC fields in order for the computer to understand.

Delimiters are characters (i.e., keystrokes made on a keyboard) that are designated by a system. When they appear, that indicates that a subfield follows. Some systems choose the $ as a delimiter; others choose the pipe symbol (to create the pipe symbol, type: *shift* plus the \ [back slash] key located above the *enter* key on standard American keyboards). In OCLC *Bibliographic Formats and Standards* Documentation, a double dagger (‡) is used; although you more than likely will not have to type the double dagger into your ILS, it might help you to recognize it. Because the MARC communications format does not specify what the delimiter is, it is up to each system to define it.

Because the delimiter only appears in the human-readable version of the record, it could theoretically be any symbol as long as it is used consistently. ILSs specify the symbol the cataloger should use as a delimiter, and they have gone out of their way to select characters to function as a delimiter that would not typically be part of the content encoded in a library record can work.

POP SINGERS AND THE ONLINE CATALOG

Pop singers have, at least for the past 20 or 30 years, chosen to write their names in interesting and clever ways. Examples include Prince who for a while wrote his name as a symbol, and Black Eyed Peas singer will.i.am, born William James Adams, Jr. P!nk took things up a notch when she used an exclamation point in the writing of her name. But it was Ke$ha who gave libraries fits when she put a $, a common delimiter in library systems, in the middle of her name. Some library systems initially recognized the second part of her name as belonging to the subfield h (i.e., $h) instead of being part of the way her name was written due to the insertion of the $.

The first bit of subfield information in a MARC record is generally included in *subfield a* (and for this reason some systems do not even bother to display the subfield a). Depending on the MARC field, there may only be a need for that subfield. Other subfields are supplied as necessary, with the delimiter and the letter or number designating the subfield preceding the content. In Figure 4.2, Apocalypse cow is subfield a. There is ISBD punctuation following the end of the title (in this case the title proper)——for more examples with ISBD punctuation in action, please see Chapters 5 and 6.

Subfield c follows subfield a in Figure 4.2. Delimiter c begins the subfield and the content of the subfield follows. For beginners, the real challenge is to remember where the ISBD punctuation goes in relationship to the delimiter. The punctuation will *always* precede the delimiter. Fields where this tends to happen a lot include the 245, the 264, and the 300. In the record for the book *Brown Girl Dreaming* by Jacqueline Woodson, we find the following 300 field:

300 _ _ $a 336 pages : $b illustrations, genealogical tables ; $c 22 cm

As with push-ups or with not screaming on roller coasters, remembering where to put the ISBD punctuation and the delimiters can be easier said than done, at least at first.

Repeatability of MARC Fields and Subfields

Sometimes, depending on the field tag, the MARC variable field may be repeatable, meaning that more than one field with the same tag can be included in a record.

020 _ _ $a 0803706197
020 _ _ $a 9780375870248

In the documentation available on the Internet from LC and from OCLC, a capital letter R is used to indicate Repeatable MARC fields (e.g., 020 R). If the MARC field is Not Repeatable, then NR will be displayed. There will be only one title and statement of responsibility (NR), for example, but there may be many subject headings (R) in a given MARC record. Catalogers do not have to guess about the repeatability of these fields; they just need to look in the documentation if there is ever a doubt. Please see the suggested readings at the end of this chapter for more information.

MARC FIELD GROUPS

MARC tags, while not entirely predictable, do follow certain patterns. Generally, MARC tags are entered into the record in number order. Catalogers tend to refer to MARC tags by their number groups. For example, any field starting with the digit one will be known by its three-digit code but might also be referred to as a 1XX by catalogers. This grouping is a kind of shorthand for describing the content that will be included in that field. The Library of Congress breaks down the MARC fields in the following way (see Table 4.1).

Table 4.1 MARC Fields and Their Explanations[4]

Field tag	Type of Field or Content Included	Plain-speak Explanation
00X	Control Fields	These are the highly encoded fields that help the computer understand more about the MARC record and about the resource being described. These fields do not print, meaning they are not shown to patrons. They can be used to refine or limit a search, however, depending on the field and the contents.
01X—09X	Numbers and Code Fields	Fields that contain data such as the ISBN, the call number, and encoded information about the library who created the record.
1XX	Primary Access Point Fields	Only one of these fields will appear in a given MARC record. This field, if included, will be the basis for alphabetizing a book on the shelf, and generally it will be the name of the author (or the first named author) if the item is a book. Names given in the 1XX will be taken from a controlled vocabulary or will be created in accordance with instructions in the content standard (i.e., this will be the *phone book* form of the name pulled from an authority record as described in Chapter 10).
20X—24X	Title and Title Related Fields	These fields record the title of the item for retrieval. They also include information such as variant titles and uniform titles.
25X—28X	Edition, Imprint, Etc. Fields	Information including the edition statement, date of publication, date of copyright, and name of publisher. Information about the imprint (i.e., publisher) is encoded in a new MARC field, 264, under RDA.
3XX	Physical Description, Etc. Fields	The 3XX fields describe physical attributes of a book such as its height in centimeters and things like color illustrations. The new 3XX fields in use in RDA, the 33X fields, now provide additional information about the resource itself and what is needed to consult it (i.e., the Content Type, Media Type, and Carrier Type information). Content Type, Media Type, and Carrier Type are encoded in the 336, 337, and 338 respectively.
4XX	Series Statement Fields	The title of a series, under certain circumstances, is recorded in this area in the 490. Series titles are searchable in library catalogs the same way that other titles are.
5XX	Note Fields	Notes about materials such as whether they contain the bibliography (and if the resources are clustered, on what page range can they be found), index, and possibly table of contents information are listed in the note field. Each note will likely have its own MARC tag.

Field tag	Type of Field or Content Included	Plain-speak Explanation
6XX	Subject Access Fields	Terms like *subject headings*, including Library of Congress subject headings and Sears subject headings, are found in the 6XX. Other terms important for access, especially in public libraries, include *genre tags*. They also are included in these fields.
70X—75X	Added Entry Fields	Like the 1XX and the 240, terms supplied in these fields tend to be created using controlled vocabularies. Added entry fields include terms for people and resources related to the material being catalogued. People might be second authors or editors, and resources might be a primary source document on which an adaptation is based.
80X—83X	Series Added Entry Fields	If there is an authorized form of the access point for a series, it needs to be included here. With some series, especially ones written for children, a single author is responsible for every book in the series. In that instance, the controlled form of the access point begins with the authorized form of the author's access point and is followed by the name of the series.
9XX	Locally Defined Fields	Sometimes it is useful to include information in a record about the local copy being held or about the creation of the record in a library's ILS. When MARC records are shared, the 9XX field is not exported. Contents in this field remain within the creator library's system.

THE STRUCTURE OF MARC RECORDS: WHAT THE USER SEES

Depending on a person's background, reading raw MARC records, even from the human-readable format, can be a challenge. To make life a bit easier on patrons, library systems display the contents of the MARC record's variable fields. Instead of showing patrons three-digit codes, however, the display only shows words as labels. The ILS also shows fields in a different order or hides some fields, potentially, and some libraries even pay for services to display cover art based on the ISBN in the catalog record.

The display is different from library to library. The choice of the words used in the content labels is up to each library, as the words used in the online display are not mandated by standards. Some academic libraries may feel that it is appropriate to use library-land cataloging jargon in their display (e.g., to label the first named author the "main entry"); this generally is not advised in any kind of library. A look at some freely available online libraries shows that most will opt for a label like "author," "creator," or "author/compiler/ editor" or some other terms patrons will likely know.

In short, MARC records cannot be "loaded" directly to the web. They need to be housed in an ILS and made available through it. Based on the ILS they choose and how they choose to set up the display, libraries may display a single MARC record very differently from another library. Indeed, MARC records *are* library data; however, they are not web-ready and are difficult to manipulate outside of the library environment.

OTHER ENCODING SCHEMAS

Although most cataloging agencies use MARC to describe physical library materials like books and audio-visual materials, MARC is not the only encoding standard used in libraries. In digital library initiatives, for example, other schemas are in use. Dublin Core (DC) and MODS are two examples of commonly used schemas that at times are used to describe the kinds of materials, especially digital, that are collected in libraries.

Dublin Core

The Dublin Core Metadata Initiative (DCMI) (http://dublincore.org/) is the *initiative* that sponsors the Dublin Core Metadata Element Set (DCMES) (http://dublincore .org/documents/dces/). The initiative, the DCMI, is an open organization that is part of a nonprofit scholarly organization, the Association for Information Science and Technology (ASIST). The element set, the DCMES, is at its most simple, a 15-element set of elements that can describe the content in electronic records. Confusingly enough, when people talk about "Dublin Core," they may be referring to the initiative or the element set, or both!

The Dublin Core project began in and is named for Dublin, Ohio, a suburb of Columbus, Ohio, where the Online Computer Library Center (OCLC) is located. Dublin Core was born in 1995, a time when the web was very young and librarians were still hoping to organize its content; it was also a time before the creation of Google, when human-made web directories like Yahoo! were a common way of finding information on the web. Dublin Core was meant to allow webmasters to become cataloging librarians of sorts by embedding very simple metadata in their web pages so that it would be possible to make sense of the content.

Dublin Core has come a long way since its origins. As with other technologies, in the end, it is not being used as it was intended and that is alright. Dublin Core, it turns out, is excellent for describing in a simple way electronic content in digital libraries and repositories. The structure of Dublin Core remains simple at heart; the most simple version is also called Simple Dublin Core. Fifteen elements can encode or describe content about a resource. Those elements are title, creator, subject, description, publisher, contributor, date, type, format, identifier, source, language, relations, coverage, and rights. No element is required in a Dublin Core record, and all can be repeated. Dublin Core's 15 elements are an ISO standard like MARC: DCMES is ISO Standard 15836:2009 of February 2009.

The only real issue with Dublin Core is that its tags are so simple that it is difficult to know what is being described. Take, for example, the element "dates." There are several kinds of dates that might be recorded: date created, date issued, date modified, and so on. However, in Simple Dublin Core, there is only one option for encoding all of these differing kinds of dates.

Qualified Dublin Core is one solution, as it includes all 15 elements of Simple Dublin Core plus three additional ones: audience, provenance, and rights holder. *Qualifiers* can also be added to each of these Qualified DC elements to indicate more precisely what kind of information is being encoded, thereby providing a solution to the dates problem identified earlier. Qualified Dublin Core (QDC) is used in a number of digital repositories.

All encoded information in QDC can be distilled down and belongs to one of the main elements for sharing or harvesting by an outside group; however, within the repository, more powerful search and description can take place. Libraries can decide on their own which fields they want to use, and, to some extent, how they will use them; this provides a great deal of flexibility in the implementation of Dublin Core.

Digital library and repository software packages like CONTENTdm, Islandora, and DSpace use Dublin Core, and the Open Archives Initiative Protocol for Metadata Harvesting (OAI-PMH) allows for electronic records in these repositories to be easily harvested for use elsewhere.

MODS and MADS

The Metadata Object Description Schema (MODS) and its companion schema, the Metadata Authority Description Schema (MADS), were created and are maintained by the Library of Congress. MODS, like Dublin Core, is used primarily in digital repositories. MODS is more detailed than Dublin Core; at the same time, it is less detailed than MARC. Generating MODS records from MARC records can be done easily since all of the detail required for MODS is already present in a standard MARC record. Another benefit to MODS is that it is XML-based. As noted, MARC is not web-ready, but XML is.

In all fairness, there is also an XML-based version of MARC, MARCXML. It does not adhere to the ISO 2709 standard that governs MARC and is clunky since it requires tags and labels. MARCXML is not used in many systems as a result, and for that reason, this book focuses its discussion of XML-based schemas on the two that are commonly used: Dublin Core and MODS. It is easier to move the content of these records into different systems and to share the content. Crosswalks work better with DC and MODS than with MARC.

Crosswalks

It is possible to take a catalog record encoded in MARC, and to convert it into another kind of schema—that is, the content can be encoded using another metadata schema based on how that content is encoded in the original MARC record. In instances where an institution's digital library or digital repository wishes to draw from items in the library catalog, there is a tendency to avoid creating a record all over again if a MARC record already exists.

Building crosswalks is not for the faint of heart, as every possibility must be weighed and considered. How *should* all of the kinds of information that can be included in a given MARC field be rendered in the target schema? With only 15 elements in DC and 18 in QDC, even with qualifiers, there are fewer tags to apply to elements than when using MARC, with its hundreds of field tags.[5] When MARC is crosswalked to DC, 200-odd tags have to be distilled down into 15 (or 18) categories. For this reason, much of the content in the MARC record will not map to a unique or equally specific field in Dublin Core. So, where should that data go?

MODS is also less precise than MARC, as the intention behind MODS is not the same as behind MARC. And, in its defense, MODS does better with other digital objects than MARC, so there are good reasons to use it in digital library environments. It is also easier to move content into different schema once the content is no longer encoded in MARC. An example is the Islandora digital repository that maps DC and MODS to each other, requiring MARC records to be converted first to one or the other.

The fact of the matter is crosswalks are possible, and with the increased amount of digital content, they are increasingly necessary. In order to create crosswalks between the library catalog and a digital library, MARC must be understood. The cataloger may be called upon to assist with the creation of crosswalks by digital repository staff eager to provide additional access to library materials. By learning and understanding more about MARC records, the cataloger will be best suited to providing guidance and assistance in these situations.

MOVING FORWARD

MARC has served the library community well for over 50 years. It is beginning to show its age. Formal complaints against MARC have been collected in recent years. Some of these include the fact that MARC is not terribly granular. Granularity in this context can mean that it is difficult to encode specific parts of catalog records so that the machine understands exactly what they are. An example of this is hyphenated names of persons. The way personal names are encoded does not clarify the distinction between a middle name or a first name, or even a last name.

The bibliographic information encoded in MARC records is in fact a kind of metadata. What is *metadata*? A standard definition of metadata is that it is structured information about other information. In terms of library cataloging, metadata tends to be descriptive information about the item's physical attributes and intellectual content, and can also be information about what is needed to access the content (computer software), who created the metadata (the name of the local librarian inputting the record in the system), or even highly encoded information within a MARC record that clarifies the version of MARC (MARC 21, UNIMARC, etc.) used to encode the record.

Since MARC records were never meant to be anything more than machine-readable, they were not designed to feed the back end of systems that display information to users through the web. They were also not meant to be created and manipulated by cataloging librarians throughout the world. Since the discussion about the deficiencies of MARC has been explored professionally for some time now, it is worth taking a few minutes to think about where library encoding standards are heading and what possible options there are at present for encoding library data.

Linked Data

The Internet used by most people today is a web of documents; pages link to each other via hypertext. This is the idea behind HTML, the Hypertext Markup Language. As things stand right now, the user has to make sense of the nature of the link. If you are reading a page and are tempted to click a link, you may have a hard time knowing 100% if you are being directed to another relevant article, to a loud video that will bother your colleagues, or to a nefarious file that will take over your desktop.

Tim Berners-Lee, the inventor of the web, began thinking of ways to make computers able to understand the nature of links and able to understand the information on the web. In 2001, he put forth the idea of the Semantic Web, a web where computers could make sense of the contents of webpages. Computers could move around from resource to resource on the proposed Semantic Web meaningfully, understanding and interacting with the content they found there.[6]

Having an idea and knowing how to put it into practice are two separate things. Berners-Lee first informally (and now formally) proposed *linked data* as the way that web content should be marked up so that computers understand it. As you may guess based on the discussion of MARC earlier in this chapter, since MARC records are not web-ready, they are not at all able to be a part of the Semantic Web.

BIBFRAME

Complaints about MARC among members of the library community date back to 2002, at least, when Roy Tennant published an article in the *Library Journal* titled "MARC Must Die."[7] Tennant likely had in mind some of the buzz about the Semantic Web when he wrote this article. And, for their part, the creators of RDA likely had both of these ideas in mind as they worked later in the decade.

RDA is built on the notion that metadata schema that allows for relationships to be made evident will be created to replace MARC. FRBR is a relationship-entity model, and its use as a basis for the content standard implies that relationships between parts of records will need to be made explicit in a way that MARC cannot. RDA cannot be fully realized until a more robust replacement for MARC exists.

In response to the need to create a new encoding scheme that adapts to RDA as well as to the web-at-large, LC announced its Bibliographic Framework Initiative, or BIBFRAME for short, in 2011. BIBFRAME (http://bibframe.org/) is roughly based on notions relating to linked data and is designed to contain library content that previously was housed in MARC. LC is very cognizant of the sheer amount of library data that exists in MARC and is working to create a standard that will be able to accommodate content from MARC records easily.

BIBFRAME is, however, working independently of RDA and is creating a BIBFRAME Model and BIBFRAME Vocabulary. A test bed is available from 2014 to 2015 for institutions to try out BIBFRAME, and email distribution lists have been set up to support communication among stakeholders. BIBFRAME may not be in use, but examples are emerging. Figures 4.4 and 4.5 show the same record encoded in two different metadata schemas. Figure 4.4 shows the cataloger's view of a MARC records: this is the kind of record that catalogers everywhere are creating today. Figure 4.5 shows the same record encoded in BIBFRAME.

One of the major concerns at present is the move from MARC to another encoding standard. Since only library vendors and open source projects stemming from libraries can understand MARC records in the first place, there is concern that new systems will be unable to import, transform, and display MARC content. Price and data loss are other concerns, among many.

```
MARC

01835cam a2200361 i 4500
001    16573501
005    20110801182216.0
008    101209t20112011nyua      b    001 0 eng
010    $a  2010051326
020    $a9781400040155
040    $aDLC$beng$cDLC$erda
042    $apcc
043    $an-us---
050 00 $aE459$b.G66 2011
082 00 $a973.7/11$222
100 1  $aGoodheart, Adam.
245 10 $a1861 :$bthe Civil War awakening /$cAdam Goodheart.
246 30 $aCivil War awakening
250    $a1st edition
260    $aNew York :$bAlfred A. Knopf,$c2011, ©2011.
300    $a481 pages :$billustrations ;$c25 cm
336    $atext$2rdacontent
337    $aunmediated$2rdamedia
338    $avolume$2rdacarrier
500    $a"This is a Borzoi book"--T.p. verso.
504    $aIncludes bibliographical references (p. [445]-456) and index.
505 0  $aPrologue : a banner at daybreak : Charleston Harbor, December 1860 -- Wide awak
e : Boston, October 1860 -- The old gentlemen : Washington, January 1861 -- Forces of na
ture : central Ohio, February 1861 -- A shot in the dark : Charleston Harbor, April 1861
-- The volunteer : lower Manhattan, April 1861 -- Gateways to the west : Carson Valley,
Nevada Territory, May 1861 -- The crossing : Washington, May 1861 -- Freedom's fortress
: Hampton Roads, Virginia, May 1861 -- Independence Day : Washington, D.C., July 1861.
651  0 $aUnited States$xHistory$yCivil War, 1861-1865$xCauses.
651  0 $aUnited States$xPolitics and government$y1861-1865.
651  0 $aUnited States$xIntellectual life$y19th century.
906    $a7$bcbc$corignew$d1$eecip$f20$gy-gencatlg
925 0  $aacquire$b2 shelf copies$xpolicy default
955    $brf08 2010-12-09$irf08 2010-12-09 (telework) to Dewey$wrd14 2010-12-09;$frg04 20
11-06-18 to CALM$trg06 2011-08-01 copy 2-3 to CALM
```

Figure 4.4 MARC Version Record.[8]

CONCLUSION

At present, MARC is what libraries use to encode the data that they have. MARC is complex and venerable; it has stood the test of time until present. In the future, it is likely that another encoding scheme that is well adapted to RDA will be created and adopted by the library community. However, no one expects that MARC will disappear right away due to the copious amount of MARC records that exist.

BIBFRAME (Turtle)

```
@prefix bf: <http://bibframe.org/vocab/> .
@prefix madsrdf: <http://www.loc.gov/mads/rdf/v1#> .
@prefix rdf: <http://www.w3.org/1999/02/22-rdf-syntax-ns#> .
@prefix rdfs: <http://www.w3.org/2000/01/rdf-schema#> .
@prefix relators: <http://id.loc.gov/vocabulary/relators/> .
@prefix xml: <http://www.w3.org/XML/1998/namespace> .
@prefix xsd: <http://www.w3.org/2001/XMLSchema#> .


<http://id.loc.gov//resources/bibs/16573501> a bf:Text,
        bf:Work ;
    bf:authorizedAccessPoint "Goodheart, Adam. 1861 :the Civil War awakening",
        "goodheartadam1861thecivilwarawakeningengworktext"@x-bf-hash ;
    bf:classification [ a bf:Classification ;
            bf:classificationEdition "22",
                "full" ;
            bf:classificationNumber "973.7/11" ;
            bf:classificationScheme <http://id.loc.gov/authorities/classSchemes/ddc> ;
            bf:label "973.7/11" ] ;
    bf:classificationLcc <http://id.loc.gov/authorities/classification/E459> ;
    bf:contentCategory <http://id.loc.gov/vocabulary/contentTypes/txt> ;
    bf:creator [ a bf:Person ;
            bf:authorizedAccessPoint "Goodheart, Adam." ;
            bf:hasAuthority [ a madsrdf:Authority ;
                    madsrdf:authoritativeLabel "Goodheart, Adam." ] ;
            bf:label "Goodheart, Adam." ] ;
    bf:derivedFrom <http://id.loc.gov//resources/bibs/16573501.marcxml.xml> ;
    bf:hasAnnotation [ a bf:Annotation ;
            bf:annotates <http://id.loc.gov//resources/bibs/16573501> ;
            bf:changeDate "2011-08-01T18:22" ;
            bf:derivedFrom <http://id.loc.gov//resources/bibs/16573501.marcxml.xml> ;
            bf:descriptionConventions <http://id.loc.gov/vocabulary/descriptionConventio
ns/isbd>,
                <http://id.loc.gov/vocabulary/descriptionConventions/rda> ;
            bf:descriptionLanguage <http://id.loc.gov/vocabulary/languages/eng> ;
            bf:descriptionSource <http://id.loc.gov/vocabulary/organizations/dlc> ;
            bf:generationProcess "DLC transform-tool:2015-01-16-T11:00:00" ] ;
    bf:hasInstance [ a bf:Instance,
                bf:Monograph ;
            bf:carrierCategory <http://id.loc.gov/vocabulary/carriers/nc> ;
            bf:contentsNote "Prologue : a banner at daybreak : Charleston Harbor, Decemb
er 1860 -- Wide awake : Boston, October 1860 -- The old gentlemen : Washington, January
1861 -- Forces of nature : central Ohio, February 1861 -- A shot in the dark : Charlesto
n Harbor, April 1861 -- The volunteer : lower Manhattan, April 1861 -- Gateways to the w
```

Figure 4.5   BIBFRAME Version Record (partial).[9]

NOTES

1. MARBI: American Library Association's ALCTS/LITA/RUSA Machine-Readable Bibliographic Information Committee in conjunction with Network Development and MARC Standards Office, Library of Congress. 1996 rev. The MARC 21 Formats: Background and Principles. 2.1. http://www.loc.gov/marc/96principl.html (Accessed February 28, 2015)

2. MARBI, 1996. para. 5.4 "The term **fixed fields** is occasionally used in MARC 21 documentation, referring either to control fields generally or to specific coded-data fields, e.g., 007 (Physical Description Fixed Field) or 008 (Fixed-Length Data Elements)."
3. MARBI, 1996.
4. MARC field groups based on http://www.loc.gov/marc/bibliographic/ecbdhome.html.
5. MARC Usage in WorldCat. 2015. OCLC Research. http://experimental.worldcat.org/marcusage/ (accessed April 9, 2015)
6. Tim Berners-Lee, James Hendler, and Ora Lassila. 2001. "The Semantic Web." *Scientific American* 284(5): 28–37.
7. Roy Tennant. 2002. "MARC Must Die." *Library Journal* 127(17): 26–27. http://lj.libraryjournal.com/2002/10/ljarchives/marc-must-die/
8. These views generated by the LC BIBFRAME Compare Tool: http://bibframe.org/tools/compare/bibid/16573501
9. Ibid.

SUGGESTED RESOURCES

MARC 21 Encoding (Bibliographic)

Bibliographic Formats and Standards. 2014. OCLC. http://oclc.org/bibformats/en.html

Furrie, Betty. 2009. *Understanding MARC Bibliographic: Machine-readable Cataloging.* 8th ed. Library of Congress Cataloging Distribution Service. Retrieved from http://www.loc.gov/marc/umb/

MARC 21 format for bibliographic data. 1999 Edition, Update No. 1 (October 2001) through Update No. 18 (April 2014). MARC Standards. Library of Congress. http://www.loc.gov/marc/bibliographic/ecbdhome.html

Dublin Core

Dublin Core Metadata Element Set (DCMES) (http://dublincore.org/documents/dces/).
The Dublin Core Metadata Initiative (DCMI) (http://dublincore.org/)

Linked Data and the Future of Library Encoding

Bibliographic Framework Initiative [BIBFRAME]. 2014. Library of Congress. http://www.loc.gov/bibframe/

Coyle, Karen. 2012. "Linked Data Tools: Connecting on the Web." *Library Technology Reports* 48(4).

BIBFRAME

Bibliographic Framework Initiative. http://www.loc.gov/bibframe/

Kroeger, Angela. (2013). "The Road to BIBFRAME: The Evolution of the Idea of Bibliographic Transition into a Post-MARC Future." *Cataloging & Classification Quarterly* 51(8): 873–890.

CHAPTER 5

RDA, the Toolkit, and Works and Expressions

In this chapter, we focus closely on RDA and on the means for consulting it: the RDA Toolkit. First we look at the Toolkit and then we apply RDA to work- and expression-level content that catalogers record in the bibliographic record.

GETTING OUR BEARINGS IN RDA

As mentioned previously, RDA is structured to align with the conceptual model called *Functional Requirements for Bibliographic Records* (FRBR).[1] Particularly, RDA focuses on the FRBR group 1 entities (group 1 = the *work, expression, manifestation,* and *item,* or WEMI). These entities assume that different descriptions are required for each level of the so-called WEMI stack; that is to say, catalogers can record descriptions pertaining to the *work* (this is a conceptual notion that focuses on the ideas in the creator's head) or to the *expression* (also a conceptual notion that includes the preparation or interpretation of the content by translations, illustrators, actors, musicians, etc.). Catalogers also record information relating to the manifestation (the run of identical items issued by the publisher) and the *item* (the object held by the library).

The illustration in Figure 5.1 demonstrates how the different parts of the WEMI model relate to one another in actual libraries. Only the items are held, but intellectually, items are related to the entities that are hierarchically above them.

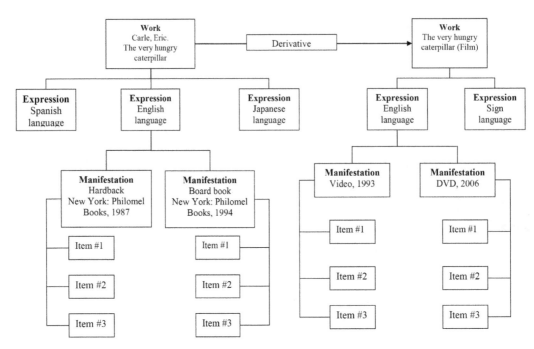

Figure 5.1   FRBR Group 1 (WEMI) Entities Example.[2]

RDA at times offers options, and not only instructions. Catalogers at the Library of Congress (LC) along with colleagues in the Program for Cooperative Cataloging (PCC) have identified in many of these instances how they will interpret the options. These decisions are included in the RDA Toolkit under the label LC-PCC PS, meaning Library of Congress-Program for Cooperative Cataloging Policy Statement. Several of the interpretations are essentially falling back on previous cataloging content standard, Anglo-American Cataloguing Rules, Second Edition (AACR2), making access to AACR2 rules through the Toolkit potentially an important feature for new catalogers starting out.[3]

RDA Core and Core If

In RDA, some elements are designated as being "core." This means that, minimally, these items must be included in the bibliographic record. For example, the date of publication is a core element. If it is available, it must be included. There are also "core if" elements. The elements become core *if* a core element is not present on an item. The copyright date is required and is core if the date of publication or the date of distribution is unknown. Most catalogers catalog beyond core, so that library users have as much information as possible about the item. Core and core if elements have been designated (Core) and (Core if) (as described further in this chapter).

Preferred Source of Information (RDA 2.2)

For each type of material, there is a specific place catalogers are supposed to look for information first. These are called preferred sources of information. If the information is not in that place, then one can look elsewhere.

For books and ebooks, the preferred source of information is the *title page,* the first page of a book where the title, author or editor, and often the publisher are listed. If the title page does not have the needed information, then catalogers look at the verso (back) of the title page (the page where copyright information is generally found) and then the cover.

For DVDs, the preferred source of information is the title screen on the viewed movie. If there is no title frame, then use the disc label, then the container. For CDs (both music and audiobooks) the preferred source of information is the disc and then the container. The cover of a serial is the preferred source of information, then the masthead, caption, and so on.

Technical Reading of an Item

As they prepare to begin cataloging, catalogers will do a technical reading of an item. A technical reading involves systematically looking over the material at hand. With books, for example, catalogers will look at the cover and the title page. They will flip briefly through the table of contents and note if there are illustrations in the book. The will check to see if there are pages of plates, an index, a bibliography, and possibly anything interesting on the back cover. They will look for series information, edition information, notable (or local) contributors (preface writers or illustrators, for example), and variant forms of the title. They might even skim through the introduction or the blurb on the back.

Then, they will open the book to the title page (generally using a ruler to hold the cover open gently), make sure their online documentation is ready (RDA Toolkit, cataloging module interface open and with ready access to URLs for the Name Authority File [NAF] and resources for providing subject access), and then will begin cataloging. The preliminary technical reading will not take long, but it is an integral part of the cataloging process. It can also be revisited at any point in the cataloging process.

Getting Our Bearings in Cataloging

In this chapter and the next, we present the content that is recorded in bibliographic records according to RDA and current practice in the United States. We use the FRBR WEMI breakdown to organize the content, beginning with work and expression in this chapter, and moving to manifestation and item and fixed field elements in the MARC record in the next chapter. For each element recorded, we provide references to RDA instructions or sets of instructions as applicable.

Where possible, we prefer to present content in MARC order since this is the way most catalogers tend to think of building records. Although the WEMI stack is helpful for thinking about how to align the different levels of content in a single bibliographic record, since all of the content is recorded in a single record at present, it is somewhat artificial to break things out the way we have. If at any point our instructions are unclear, consider going to the example of RDA and MARC records in Appendix 1 to see some of these elements in action.

USING THE RDA TOOLKIT

The RDA Toolkit (http://access.rdatoolkit.org/) is the primary way to consult the RDA instructions. The Toolkit is not free—it requires an annual subscription based on the number of users at the institution.[4] If your institution is a member of a library consortium such as Amigos, it might be possible to negotiate a reduced rate through the consortium. A free trial[5] is possible as well.

A fair amount of support is available on the website. RDA Toolkit Essentials (http://www.rdatoolkit.org/essentials) offers regular webinars and slides and videos from past webinars for free. Training materials are available from a number of other institutions, but these tend to be for users who were proficient in the previous cataloging content standard, AACR2.

Once inside the Toolkit, there is a Help button at the bottom of every screen that links to the Toolkit Help; the Help documentation has the following chapters in its table of contents: Logging in and Creating Profiles; Navigating RDA Toolkit; Search Tips; User-Contributed Content; Support and Feedback Options; and Administration System.

Next we explain enough about using the Toolkit that you should be comfortable giving it a try on your own, knowing that you can always turn to the Help screens if necessary.

Getting Started with the Toolkit

On the main page of the Toolkit, there is a menu on the left-hand side with three tabs. The first tab, RDA, is the most important. We will describe it more in the next section.

The second tab, Tools, includes information about RDA-related element sets and sample records. It also includes workflows that will be of assistance to novice Toolkit users. In the Global Workflows section of the Tools tab, choose the workflow for the kind of material you are cataloging and follow the instructions. There are also mappings in this tab. Choose the RDA Mappings and then select *RDA to MARC Bibliographic Mapping* to find a comprehensive, field-by-field map of MARC fields and their instructions in RDA.

The third tab is the Resources tab. It includes Library of Congress-Program for Cooperative Cataloging Policy Statements (LC-PCC PS). As mentioned, they are also linked up to the RDA instructions in the RDA tab. It also includes a link to the former cataloging code, AACR2. Though you will not want to read it cover to cover, AACR2 might provide some additional background if RDA does not provide sufficient rationale or explanation.

RDA, the Resource

RDA is currently composed of 32 chapters, with four additional chapters slated for completion at a later date. From the main RDA tab, the first chapter and subsequent sections (groups of chapters) are evident. A small plus symbol to the left indicates when content can be expanded. That expanded content is shown in the main window in the center of the screen.

Chapter 0 serves as the introduction. Section 1: Recording Attributes of Manifestation & Item follows. It contains chapters 1–4: chapter 1, General Guidelines on Recording Attributes of Manifestations and Items; chapter 2 Identifying Manifestations and Items; chapter 3 Describing carriers; and chapter 4, Providing Acquisition and Access Information. These chapters will be the primary focus of the discussion in the next chapter of our *Crash Course*.

The next section, Section 2: Recording Attributes of Work & Expression, contains three chapters, 5–7. They are: chapter 5, General Guidelines on Recording Attributes of Works and Expressions; chapter 6, Identifying Works and Expressions, and chapter 7, Describing Content. These chapters will be the primary focus of the remainder of this chapter in our *Crash Course*.

Section 3: Recording Attributes of Person, Family, & Corporate Body contains four chapters. They are: chapter 8, General Guidelines on Recording Attributes of Persons, Families, and Corporate Bodies; chapter 9, Identifying Persons; chapter 10, Identifying Families, and chapter 11, Identifying Corporate Bodies. These are discussed in Chapter 7 of this *Crash Course.*

Section 4: Recording Attributes of Concept, Object, Event & Place is composed of five chapters, chapters 12–16. Those chapters are: chapter 12, General Guidelines on Recording Attributes of Concepts, Objects, Events, and Places, chapter 13, Identifying Concepts; chapter 14, Identifying Objects; chapter 15, Identifying Events; and chapter 16, Identifying Places. These chapters are mostly concerned with subject headings, which we discuss in Chapter 8. However, with the exception of chapter 16, Identifying Places, the chapters are just placeholders and will be developed further at a later date.

Sections 5, 6, 7, 8, and 9 help catalogers understand when and how relationships need to be recorded in bibliographic records. Some of these will be addressed in this and the following chapter as well.

Finally, RDA consists of 12 appendices that give instructions on how to record content in the bibliographic record. Appendix D.2.1 Mapping of MARC 21 Bibliographic to RDA provides in-depth examples of RDA content being encoded in MARC 21. There is also a glossary and an index.

Searching in RDA

Looking up instructions in the RDA Toolkit can happen two ways. First, it is possible to browse based on the structure of the sections and chapters. Second, keywords/character strings can be searched either using the RDA Quick Search box available at the top of the pages or through the Advanced Search page, available by clicking the magnifying glass also at the top of the pages.

IN THEORY AND IN PRACTICE

In theory, RDA is based on the WEMI model, as put forth in the FRBR conceptual model. In practice, however, MARC cannot meet the needs of RDA. A new encoding standard is needed to support the full potential of RDA's implementation of the WEMI model, including the need to make relationships explicit. The cataloging community is working with vendors to imagine what cataloging might look like in the future under RDA once MARC is replaced. LC is working with Zepheira to produce BIBFRAME, an XML-based schema that will go beyond MARC. Catalogers can practice inputting information based on RDA into the BIBFRAME Editor (BFE) http://bibframe.org/tools/ or into the BIBFRAME Scribe prototype http://editor.bibframe.zepheira.com/static/index.html developed by Zepheira.

At present, however, catalogers still use MARC, and systems need to support the millions of records in MARC that exist. This is an exciting time for library encoding, as the change in schema that RDA requires is on the horizon.

In this book, we show you how encoding looks in MARC, since that is the standard that is currently in use. We are also as clear as possible about when we are referring to MARC fields, RDA instructions, and chapters in this book. There are already a fair number of acronyms in cataloging (see Figure 5.2), and our intention is to make them as easily understood as possible in practice.

©2015 Mya Gosling   www.goodticklebrain.com

Figure 5.2   RDA Training, Part 3: A Humorous Look at Cataloging Acronyms, Both Real and Imagined.

Some tricky notions to represent in MARC are the different levels of content (e.g., work-level, expression-level), and some of the RDA content is not really effectively encoded in MARC at all. Additionally, some fields that catalogers include in MARC do not have instructions in RDA. Cataloging involves merging a number of different standards, all maintained by different groups! Next we discuss work-level and expression-level content and share best practices for including it in MARC.

WORK-LEVEL CONTENT

In FRBR, *work* is a conceptual notion that can go on to be *expressed* in a number of ways (we will discuss expressions in the next section of this chapter). Work-level records can be a little difficult to understand because there is nothing physical to correspond to them. There is also some debate as to whether the work-level record is an authority record (authority records will be discussed more in Chapter 7 of this book) or a bibliographic record. For now, information about the work goes in the bibliographic record. The following section examines the work-level content recorded in the bibliographic record.

Title of the Work (RDA 6.2; See Also 6.14 Title of a Musical Work) (Core)

The title at the work-level is the "preferred title for the work" (formerly known as the uniform title). In MARC this title will go in the 240 if there in an author for the work (such as for Leo Tolstoy's *War and Peace*). The title will go in a 130 field if there is not an author, such as for religious works like the Koran or the Bible or for pre-1501 anonymous works like Beowulf.

240 10 $a Voi′na i mir. $l English

130 0_ $a Bible. $p Thessalonians. $l Italian

For items that have been published many times in various ways such as the Bible or Shakespeare's plays, the work-level title will come from an authority record. This title has to collocate all iterations of the work, regardless of what is on a particular item's title page. An example is Mark Twain's Huck Finn. Any number of titles may appear on the title page, including in foreign languages. A work-level title allows for the collocation or grouping of these items no matter what appears on the title page.

For the majority of works that have only one or two iterations, there will not be an authority record, nor will there be a 130/240. The cataloger will just use the title on the item in the 245 (described in Chapter 6 in the manifestation-level content section).

Creator (RDA 19.2) (Core[6])

The author has the main responsibility for the intellectual content of a work. Most works will only have one author, but there could be multiple authors listed. The work's author will be in the 100 Main Entry—Personal Name field of a MARC record, with additional authors being in the 700s (Added Entry—Personal Name). People with other types of responsibility for the intellectual content (editors, actors, translators, etc.) will be listed as expression-level content (RDA 20.0), also in the 700 Added Entry—Personal Name.

Both the work-level and expression-level contents make use of the 1XX, 6XX, and 7XX fields. The 1XX, 6XX, and 7XX fields, however, are access points based on the description. For information on constructing/using authorized access points, see Chapter 7 in this book. For information on subject headings, see Chapter 8 in this book.

Other Information

Other information can be included at the work-level; much of it is required only under certain circumstances. Possible information is the Form of Work (RDA 6.3) (Core if[7]), Date of Work (RDA 6.4) (Core if[8]), Place of Origin of the Work (RDA 6.5) (Core if[9]), and Other Distinguishing Characteristic of the Work (RDA 6.6) (Core if[10]). Printed music will include the Medium of Performance of Musical Content (RDA 7.21), Numeric Designation of a Musical Work (RDA 6.16) (Core if[11]), and Key (RDA 6.17) (Core if[12]). Currently, this information may appear on a title or name/title authority record, and it may or may not become a part of the preferred title for the work.

EXPRESSION-LEVEL CONTENT

In the FRBR way of looking at things, the expression is the preparation or interpretation of the content by translations, illustrators, actors, musicians, and others. Expression-level content in cataloging is generally concerned with the illustrations that accompany works and with the language in which they appear, although other information like content type will also be considered here.

Illustrative Content (RDA 7.15) (Core Element for LC[13])

Illustrations can distinguish one expression from the next. Illustration information appears at present in the 300 $b of the MARC record (with 300 being Physical Description and $b being Other physical details). If the illustrator and the author are not one and the same, the access point for the illustrator will be recorded in a 700 field. For instance, Maurice Sendak both wrote and illustrated *Where the Wild Things Are,* so there would only be a 100 Main Entry—Personal Name for him as author and illustrator, no 700 Added Entry—Personal Name.

However, *Saint George and the Dragon* was written by Margaret Hodges, but illustrated by Trina Schart Hyman. In this case Hodges is the 100 Main Entry—Personal Name since she was the creator, and Hyman will be in a 700 Added Entry—Personal Name as illustrator. Since Hyman received a Caldecott Award for her illustrations, this information will also be noted in a 586 Awards Note (see the section on awards for more details).

Different illustrations/illustrators of a work make for different expressions. This does not happen often, but one example would be the *Little House* series by Laura Ingalls

Wilder. The series was originally illustrated by Helen Sewell, but later editions were illustrated by Garth Williams. The physical description section in the next chapter gives further information on recording the 300 $b.

Content Type (RDA 6.9) (Core)

Content type was discussed earlier in Chapter 3. The list of content types is in RDA 6.9.1.3 Recording Content Type (Table 6.1). These will go in field 336 of the MARC cataloging record.

(book) 336 _ _ $a text $b txt $2 rdacontent
(DVD) 336 _ _ $a two-dimensional moving image $b tdi $2 rdacontent
(CD) 336 _ _ $a performed music $b prm $2 rdacontent

Language of the Expression (6.11) (Core)

Practically speaking, *English* is not recorded in a human-readable way in the bibliographic record if the item is in English and its original language is English. For items in an original non-English language, this information will be recorded in a 546 field.

MARC 546 Language Note

If an item is not in English or if there are multiple languages, it should be noted. Translation notes are coded 500 in the MARC record.

546 _ _ $a Text in Spanish and English.
546 _ _ $a In French with English subtitles.
546 _ _ $a Closed-captioned.
546 _ _ $a Open captioned.
546 _ _ $a Signed in American Sign Language.
546 _ _ $a Audio-described.

For a translated item, the translated language will be added to the preferred title for the work. A note about the translation can be added in a 500 General Note field but is not required. An access point for the translator will be added as a 700 Added Entry—Personal Name.

240 10 $a Trois mousquetaires [this is the original novel in French]
240 10 $a Trois mousquetaires. $l English [this is the translated novel, in English]

Additionally, coded information about the language(s) used can be included in the 041 Language Code using the MARC Code List for Languages (http://www.loc.gov/marc/languages/). This field can be used if there are multiple languages in an item or if the item is a translation.

Supplementary Content (RDA 7.16) (Core Element for LC[14])

Supplementary content uses the MARC note fields for recording information about bibliographical references. Footnotes, endnotes, bibliographies, filmographies, and so on are all considered bibliographical references. If they are all found in one place, include the page numbers in parentheses in a 504 Bibliography and so on. *Note:* If there is also an index, it will be noted with the note about the bibliography in the 504 instead of in a separate 500 General Note. If there is an index but no bibliographical references, the index will be noted in a 500 General Note.

(no references) 500 _ _ $a Includes index.

(no index, references throughout) 504 _ _ $a Includes bibliographical references.

(no index, references grouped) 504 _ _ $a Includes bibliographical references (pages 94–95).

(references grouped) 504 _ _ $a Includes bibliographical references (pages 310–325) and index.

(more than one index, references throughout) 504 _ _ $a Includes bibliographical references and indexes.

(no index, filmography grouped) 504 _ _ $a Includes filmography (pages 150–152).

Performers, Narrators, and/or Presenters (RDA 7.23)

Names of participants such as performers, narrators, and/or presenters are not core, but are helpful. They will go in 511 Participant or Performer Note field for description. If the performers, narrators, and/or presenters are considered to be important to the expression and need access points to facilitate retrieval, the access points for the names will be recorded in the cataloging record as 700s (names of people) or 710 (names of corporate bodies). See Chapter 7 in this book for more information about access points.

For DVDs, the 511 will record information about the cast or any other person that appears or whose voice is heard onscreen. For music CDs, catalogers use the 511 for performers if these performers were not included in the statement of responsibility (see manifestation-level information in Chapter 6). For audiobooks, catalogers use the 511 to record the narrator if he or she was not included in the statement of responsibility. The first indicator 1 will, in correctly configured ILSs, display the label "Cast" to patrons. Accordingly, if the names recorded in the 511 are the names of the cast, use the first indicator 1. If the people listed are narrators and other (i.e., not "cast"), then use the first indicator 0. Nothing will display to the patrons if the first indicator 0 is used. We know this because in the MARC documentation, we see that for the first indicator 0, "No display constant generated."[15]

511 1_ $a Ewan McGregor, Natalie Portman, Hayden Christensen, Ian McDiarmid, Samuel L. Jackson, Christopher Lee, Anthony Daniels, Kenny Baker, Frank Oz.

511 0_ $a Narrator, Don Wescott.

Artistic and/or Technical Credit (RDA 7.24)

Non-performers can also contribute to an item, though their inclusion in the bibliographic record is not core. The cataloger records information about them in the 508 Creation/Production Credits Note field. For DVDs/Blu-rays, the executive producer, director of photography, editor, and music composer will be recorded in the 508. Other artistic and/or technical contributors may be included in the 508 if important to the work. For instance, the choreographer of a dance work or the animator of an animated work should be included. Less significant positions, like casting director, hair/make-up, special effects, and costume designers, are up to cataloger's judgment but are generally not included.

For CDs, it is best practice to include producers, directors (artistic or music), and editors in the 508.

> 508 _ _ $a Executive producer, George Lucas ; director of photography, David Tattersall ; editor, Ben Burtt ; music, John Williams.
>
> 508 _ _ $a Executive producer, Patricia Shitcher ; director of photography, Tobias Schliessler ; editor, Virginia Katz ; music, Henry Krieger ; lyrics, Tom Eyen ; choreographer, Fatima Robinson.
>
> 508 _ _ $a Writer, Carolyn Frank ; music, Oscar Aguayo, Carolyn Frank.

Award (RDA 7.28)

If the item has been nominated or won any awards, these should be recorded in a 586 Awards Note in the bibliographic record. If an item has been out for a while before the cataloger receives it or if the library is buying additional and/or replacement copies, award information may already be on the item (the publisher may have added a sticker to the front cover, for example). However, it is often necessary to go back and put this information in the catalog record after the item has been cataloged. Common lists to check are Caldecott, Newberry, Oscar, Emmy, and Grammy. Also, any state or local awards lists that children might be required to read can be consulted.

In addition to the awards listed here, there are many other awards given out. Which you choose to include in the bibliographic record is a matter of local policy and needs. For those awards you routinely add to records, make sure that you use a standardized wording and that reference desk workers know what it is so that help patrons find these items. Another possibility is to also add the awards as an 830 (series) so that they can be found in a title search, rather than having to do a keyword search only.

> 586 _ _ $a Caldecott Medal, 1999.
> 586 _ _ $a Academy Award for Best Picture, 2002.

Other Information

As with the work-level content, Date of Expression (6.10) (Core if[16]) and other distinguishing characteristics may be recorded as needed to differentiate an expression. Subject heading information can also be included on expression-level records. See Chapter 8 for further information on subject headings.

CONCLUSION

In this section, we explored how RDA can be used to describe the work- and expression-level content of a number of kinds of library materials. RDA insists on the different levels of description that can be recorded for works, expressions, manifestations, and items (WEMI)—all of that content must be contained in a single catalog record at present. Currently, most integrated library systems (ILSs) only allow for one manifestation-level record that includes additional information. ILS vendors, however, are working toward systems that will be able to accommodate compatible records for all of the WEMI levels. Future systems might have one work-level record for *Gone with the Wind,* and, to it, will attach different expression-level records associated with the manifestations produced that represent the items held.

In the next chapter, we describe how content more directly related to the item on the cataloger's desk is encoded for inclusion in the bibliographic record.

NOTES

1. International Federation of Library Associations, & Institutions. Section on Cataloguing. Standing Committee. (1998). *Functional Requirements for Bibliographic Records: Final Report* (Vol. 19). IFLA Study Group on the Functional Requirements for Bibliographic Records (Ed.). KG Saur Verlag Gmbh & Company. http://www.ifla.org/files/assets/cataloguing/frbr/frbr_2008.pdf (Accessed March 1, 2015)

2. Based on an illustration in an article by Allison Carlyle: Carlyle, Allison. 2006. "FRBR and the Bibliographic Universe, or, How to Read FRBR as a Model." *Library Resources & Technical Services,* 50(4): 270.

3. See Peter H. Lisius. 2015. "AACR2 to RDA: Is Knowledge of Both Needed during the Transition Period?" *Cataloging & Classification Quarterly* 53(1): 40–70.

4. RDA Toolkit Pricing: http://www.rdatoolkit.org/pricing

5. RDA Toolkit Free Trial Request Form: http://access.rdatoolkit.org/freetrial

6. According to RDA 19.2, only the creator having principal responsibility or the first-named creator is required.

7. RDA 6.3: "Form of work is a core element when needed to differentiate a work from another work with the same title or from the name of a person, family, or corporate body."

8. RDA 6.4: "Date of work is a core element to identify a treaty. Date of work is also a core element when needed to differentiate a work from another work with the same title or from the name of a person, family, or corporate body."

9. RDA 6.5: "Place of origin of the work is a core element when needed to differentiate a work from another work with the same title or from the name of a person, family, or corporate body."

10. RDA 6.6: "Other distinguishing characteristic of the work is a core element when needed to differentiate a work from another work with the same title or from the name of a person, family, or corporate body."

11. RDA 6.16: "Numeric designation is a core element when needed to differentiate a musical work from another work with the same title. It may also be a core element when identifying a musical work with a title that is not distinctive."

12. RDA 6.17: "Key is a core element when needed to differentiate a musical work from another work with the same title. It may also be a core element when identifying a musical work with a title that is not distinctive."

13. LC-PCC PS for 7.15: "Illustrative content is a core element for LC for resources intended for children."

14. LC-PCC PS for 7.16: "Supplementary content is a core element for LC for indexes and bibliographies in monographs."

15. MARC 511—Participant or Performer Note (R). 2001. Library of Congress. http://www.loc.gov/marc/bibliographic/bd511.html (accessed April 9, 2015)

16. RDA 6.10: "Date of expression is a core element when needed to differentiate an expression of a work from another expression of the same work."

SUGGESTED RESOURCE

Teaching and Training. 2015. RDA Toolkit. American Library Association, Canadian Library
Association, and CILIP: Chartered Institute of Library and Information Professionals. Available online: http://www.rdatoolkit.org/training.

CHAPTER 6

RDA: Manifestations and Items

This is the chapter where we get down to brass tacks. Here, we will be using RDA to describe in a consistent way the items that cross our desks as catalogers. Those items can be books, DVDs, electronic files, or even kits that are collections of hand puppets. Specifics of cataloging each kind of carrier, in RDA parlance, can be studied in depth in other books about cataloging. In this *Crash Course* book, we will focus on the basics of describing books and will give some information about other common resources.

The examples shown here include ISBD (International Standard Bibliographic Description) punctuation, specialized punctuation that makes the contents of cataloging records more easily eye-readable by humans. These are punctuation-based dividers that signal different areas of information. RDA itself does not require the use of ISBD, but it is still being used in the current MARC environment.

We begin with a look at manifestation-level content, content that rolls off a publisher's printing press. This is a fairly long section. Again, we present the content in MARC number order to the extent possible, and invite you at any time to look at the end result in Appendix A. There, we have a section of RDA content, organized numerically by instruction number. We also have MARC records, shown as they would appear in a cataloging module of an integrated library system (ILS).

We end this chapter with a short section on cataloging items and a *crash course* in encoding the fixed fields in MARC records.

MANIFESTATION-LEVEL CONTENT

In FRBR, the manifestation is the physical embodiment of an expression of a work. The manifestation-level content contains the bulk of the information in the bibliographic record. New bibliographic records are created any time a resource is published in a different format (hardback versus paperback, DVD versus Blu-ray) or is issued by a different publisher. Items that have simply been reprinted do not trigger the creation of a new bibliographic record. Unlike the work- and expression-level contents, which contain the authorized versions of access points, most of the manifestation-level content is descriptive, which means that it is transcribed exactly from the item.

Title (RDA 2.3) and Statement of Responsibility (RDA 2.4) (Core)

This information is input in the 245 of a MARC record and is divided into three parts: the main title, other title information, and statement(s) of responsibility. The 245 always ends with a period.

The Title Proper (RDA 2.3.2) (Core) is the main title of the item; it is recorded in the 245 $a.

The Other Title Information (RDA 2.3.4) is usually the subtitle; Other Title Information is preceded by a space-colon-space and is recorded in the 245 $b. Not all items will have a subtitle, so not all bibliographic records will have a 245 $b and the preceding ISBD space-colon-space.

The statement(s) of responsibility records those people or corporate bodies listed on the title page that have created the work in some way. These names will follow an ISBD space-slash-space and will be given in the 245 $c.

For books, the statement of responsibility includes authors, editors, illustrators, compilers, translators, and so on. For DVDs, writers, producers, and directors (others will be included elsewhere). For audiobooks, author(s) and narrator(s). For music, this will be the artist/band/performing group if all the songs are performed by the same entity or the composer, if they were all composed by the same person.

Catalogers record Title and Statement of Responsibility information exactly as given on the title page, when it comes to wording and spelling. However, it is possible to change or add punctuation (beyond the ISBD punctuation) to help with clarity—this is often necessary because the item will use typography and placement, which cannot be replicated in the bibliographic record.

RDA states in Transcription (RDA 1.7) that catalogers should use the capitalization of the item, but alternatively, catalogers can use an "in-house guidelines for capitalization, punctuation, numerals, symbols, abbreviations, etc." (RDA 1.7.1). Most catalogers choose the alternative and use the same capitalization rules as AACR2. In the 245, capitalize the first word and any proper nouns. All other words are lowercase.

245 10 $a Diary of a worm / $c by Doreen Cronin ; pictures by Harry Bliss.
245 00 $a Star wars. $n Episode II, $p Attack of the clones / $c presented by Twentieth Century Fox ; directed by George Lucas ; screenplay by George Lucas and Jonathan Hales ; story by George Lucas ; produced by Rick McCallum.
245 10 $a Start smart songs for 1's, 2's, and 3's : $b brain-building activities / $c by Pam Schiller.
245 00 $a Preparing principals for a changing world : $b lessons from effective school leadership programs / $c Linda Darling-Hammond, Debra Meyerson,

Michelle LaPointe, Margaret Terry Orr ; in collaboration with Margaret Barber [and seven others].

Variant Title (RDA 2.3.6)

Variant titles are those titles "associated with a resource that differs from a title recorded as the title proper" and others.[1] They have two types; the first are titles found on the item, but in a different form than what is on the preferred source (i.e., the title page of a book). The second type of variant titles are variations of the title that someone might reasonably look up when doing a title search, but that do not match, character for character, the title on the title page. This latter category includes spelling out a-n-d for an ampersand, spelling out numbers, and alternate spellings. It can also include portions of the title/subtitle that may be memorable on their own. The 245 title is recorded as always, and additional variant titles are recorded in the 246 field.

246 14 $a State publications monthly checklist

246 1_ $i Title on container: $a Dr. Seuss's The 5000 fingers of Dr. T
246 3_ $a Five thousand fingers of Dr. T
246 3_ $a Dr. Seuss's The five thousand fingers of Dr. T
246 3_ $a Doctor Seuss's The 5000 fingers of Dr. T

Edition Statement (RDA 2.5) (Core)

Edition statements are core elements of RDA records. They are very important and should always be included in the bibliographic record and transcribed exactly from the item. Edition statements can be numbered (first, tenth, etc.) or named (anniversary, teacher's, etc.). Capitalize the first word and any proper nouns and end with a period. For audiobooks, abridged and unabridged are considered edition statements. For DVDs, widescreen and full screen are considered edition statements only if they appear with the word "version." Edition goes in the 250 field.

250 _ _ $a Second edition.
250 _ _ $a Revised edition.
250 _ _ $a Southwest edition.
250 _ _ $a Anniversary edition.
250 _ _ $a Revised ninth edition.
250 _ _ $a Widescreen version.

Publication Statement (RDA 2.8) (Core[2])

Three kinds of publication information are recorded in bibliographic records: the city of publication, the publisher, and dates of publication and copyright. The publication statement can also include information on the distributor and manufacturer if the information is present on the item. Publication information goes in the 264 field.

Place of Publication (RDA 2.8.2): The city and state associated with the item's publication is recorded in the 264 $a. Place of publication information is usually given on the title page, but sometimes must come from the title page verso (i.e., the back side of the title page where the copyright information is located). If a place of publication is not identified, bracket your best guess (e.g., [Toronto]) to indicate that you, the cataloger, supplied the information, and move on. LC-PCC PS insists on the importance of place of publication information, so if you have to take a guess, that is preferable to leaving this information blank.

> 264 _1 $a [London?]

Publisher's Name (RDA 2.8.4): The publisher's name is recorded in the 264 $b. The publisher is almost always listed on the title page of books. For both the city and publisher, more than one might be listed on the resource. In both cases, only the first one listed is required to be recorded in the bibliographic record. If there is more than one listed, you can record them, but then they must *all* be recorded. So if there are five cities of publication, then you can only list the first one or list all five. You cannot choose just two or three.

Date of Publication (RDA 2.8.6): Dates are very important. RDA requires a publication date in the 264 _ 1 $c. A date of publication is "a date associated with the publication, release, or issuing of a resource" (RDA 2.8.6.1). Dates of publication tend to be given on the title page near the publisher name.

A date of publication is different from a copyright date since a copyright date is "is a date associated with a claim of protection under copyright or a similar regime."[3] The two, it turns out, are very different kinds of dates, and RDA is most interested in the date of publication! The date of publication goes at the end of the Publication Statement in the 264 _1 in the $c.

> 264 _ 1 $a London ; $a New York : $b McGraw-Hill, $c 2004.
> 264 _ 1 $a Minneapolis : $b Judy/Instructo, $c [1979]
> 264 _ 1 $a Westport, Conn. : $b Greenwood Press, $c 1983.

If there is no publication date on the item, the cataloger will infer the date of publication based on the copyright date (probably taken from the back side of the title page). Bracket the copyright date as an inferred date of publication.

> 264 _ 1 $a [Toronto] : $b National Film Board of Canada, $c [1994]
> 264 _ 1 $a New York, N.Y. : $b RCA Victor, $c [2000]

If there is no date on the item at all (i.e., the Date of Publication Not Identified in a Single-Part Resource [RDA 2.8.6.6]), make your best guess, bracket the date, supply a question mark in brackets if you are really not sure, and move on.

> 264 _ 1 $a Oxford : $b Oxford University Press ; $a New York : $b Berkeley
>   Books, $c [1998?]

For audiobooks and DVDs, use the date of the item in its present form. If the date of the original is important, this information can be put in a note (see below for more information about notes in bibliographic records). Recorded sound does not have a copyright per se; instead, it has a phonogram date. These dates will be preceded by the phonogram symbol, Ⓟ.

Copyright Date (2.11) (Core if[4])

Copyright dates are recorded in the 264 _ 4 $c following the copyright symbol, ©. Copyright dates are only required if publication and distribution dates are not identified in the 264 _1. The copyright symbol is used; it can generally be created by typing an opening parenthesis, the lowercase letter c, and the closing parenthesis with no spaces. When cataloging music, you may record a phonogram symbol (Ⓟ) and date instead of a copyright symbol and date.

    264 _ 4 $c ©1979
    264 _ 4 $c ©1954
    264 _ 4 $a Ⓟ1956

Physical Description

The physical description has four parts: the extent of the item (RDA 3.4), other physical details (i.e., illustrative content RDA 7.15), dimensions (RDA 3.5), and accompanying materials (i.e., related manifestation RDA 27.1). This information goes in the 300 field of the bibliographic record.

Extent (RDA 3.4) (Core)

The cataloger records information about the units making up the resource in the MARC 300 $a. For books this is the number of pages; users should be able to understand how thick the book is based on this field.

Many books for adults have introductory pages with Roman numerals and then start the numbering over again with Arabic numerals for the main portion of the text; in this case, the largest number of both sets of numbering is recorded in the 300 $a.

If there are pages of pictures that fall outside the normal numbering, these are called plates and should be noted since they contribute to the thickness of the book. Record as, for example, "16 pages of plates" or, if you have to count them, as, for example, "8 unnumbered pages of plates." In most books, plates will be found in groupings of 8 or a multiple thereof.

If the book does not have page numbers, you can either record it as "1 volume (unpaged)" or count the number of pages yourself, for example, "22 unnumbered pages."

For ebooks, use, for example, "1 online resource (315 pages)."

For DVDs, CDs, and CD/DVD-ROMs, you will include the number of discs in the 300 $a.

For current serials, just use "volumes." If the serial is complete, you can put the number of volumes (not issues or number of individual pieces).

Illustrative Content (RDA 7.15)

Technically, illustrative content is expression-level content. Illustrative content is recorded in the 300 $b, so we have decided to discuss it here with the other elements of the MARC 300 field.

If a book or serial has illustrative matter, use the term *illustrations*. Note here if some or all of the illustrations are in color (see Colour Content [RDA 7.17] for examples). RDA uses "colour," but LC practice is to use the U.S. spelling.[5]

If there are specific types of illustrations per the alternatives at Recording Illustrative Content (RDA 7.15.1.3), these can be also be listed in the 300 $b. Examples include maps, portraits, and music. Math equations/symbols and tables consisting only of text are not considered illustrations. Illustrated title pages, chapter headings, and author portraits are ignored.

For DVDs/Blu-rays, record that the item has sound (use silent only if there is absolutely no sound whatsoever) and then if an item is in color, black and white, or a mix.

The sound characteristics of CDs used to be given in the MARC 300, but it is now preferred that this information go in a MARC 344 field. For most CDs, this would mean recording if an item is analog or digital and if it is mono or stereo. The types of information entered into the 344 comes from lists in RDA 3.16.1.3–3.16.9.3.

Dimensions (RDA 3.5)

Dimensions are supplied in the MARC 300 $c.

For books or serials, per Recording Dimensions (RDA 3.5.1.3), measure the height of the book in centimeters. Always round up to the next whole centimeter. Information on recording Volumes (RDA 3.5.1.4.14) states that if an item is longer (wider) than it is tall or the width is less than half the height of the book, give both the length and the height. For Resources Consisting of More Than One Carrier (RDA 3.5.1.6), if the height of a serial has changed over time, give the height as a range..

For all types of discs, LC practice is to "Record the diameter of discs in inches" even though RDA's examples use centimeters.[6] In the United States, catalogers give the size as 4 3/4 in.

For ebooks and other digital materials, do not include anything.

300 _ _ $a 327 pages : $b illustrations, facsimiles, maps, portraits. ; $c 20 x 8 cm
300 _ _ $a 246 pages, 32 unnumbered pages of plates : $b illustrations ; $c 32 cm
300 _ _ $a 5 volumes : $b illustrations ; $c 28 cm
300 _ _ $a 31 unnumbered pages. : $b color illustrations ; $c 19 x 23 cm
300 _ _ $a 1 videodisc (55 min.) : $b DVD video, sound, color ; $c 4 ¾ in. OR
300 _ _ $a 1 DVD video (55 min.) : $b sound, color ; $c 4 ¾ in.
300 _ _ $a 1 audio disc : $b digital, CD audio ; $c 4 3/4 in.

Once you begin to catalog DVDs regularly, you may find yourself thinking in cataloging terms at inappropriate times, such as in discussions with non-catalogers. See Figure 6.1 for a humorous illustration of one of the risks.

Related Manifestation (RDA 27.1) aka Accompanying Materials

Most items do not have accompanying materials, but some do. Accompanying materials are recorded in the 300 $e of the bibliographic record. Examples of accompanying

©2015 Mya Gosling   www.goodticklebrain.com

Figure 6.1   RDA Training, Part 7: A Risk of Cataloging Too Many DVDs.

materials are discs or some type of illustration folded in a pocket of a book. Additionally, CDs and DVDs/Blu-rays may have a guide or program notes inserted in the container.

300 _ _ $a xix, 271 pages : $b illustrations ; $c 21 cm + $e 1 sound disc (4 ¾ in.)

Media Type (RDA 3.2) (Not Core) and Carrier Type (RDA 3.3) (Core)

These were discussed in Chapter 3. The Media Type is found in RDA 3.2.1.3 Recording Media Type (RDA Table 3.1) and is input in field 337. The Carrier Type is found in RDA 3.3.1.3 Recording Carrier Type and is input in field 338. The Carrier Types are grouped by Media Type. When choosing a Carrier Type, it must come from the list that matches the Media Type.

(book) 337 _ _ $a unmediated $b n $2 rdamedia
(DVD) 337 _ _ $a video $b v $2 rdamedia
(CD) 337 _ _ $a audio $b s $2 rdamedia

(book) 338 _ _ $a volume $b nc $2 rdacarrier
(DVD) 338 _ _ $a videodisc $b vd $2 rdacarrier
(CD) 338 _ _ $a audio disc $b sd $2 rdacarrier

Numbering of Serials (RDA 2.6) (Core[7])

The first issue of a serial should be recorded if known. If a serial is complete, the last issue should also be recorded. These are recorded in MARC field 362.

362 1_ $a Began with: 2000; ceased with: 2004.
362 1_ $a Began with: 1974.
362 1_ $a Ceased in 1980s?
362 1 _ $a Began with: Volume 6(5) (May 1991); ceased with: Volume 20(1) (spring 2005).
362 1_ $a Began with: #1 (August 4, 1986) ; ceased with: Volume 3, number 4 (April 1, 1988).

Series Statement (RDA 2.12) (Core)

If an item has a series, that information needs to be on the bibliographic record. When transcribing the title of the series directly from the item, the transcribed title will go in the 490 field. The authorized form will go in the 800, 810, or 830 and will be discussed further in Chapter 7. If a series has numbering, include it.

490 1_ $a Dear America
490 1_ $a Forgotten pioneers series
490 1_ $a The best of Broadway ; $v volume VI
490 1_ $a Architectural design, $x 0003–8504 ; volume 82, number 3
490 1_ $a Practical parenting ; $v 9
490 1_ $a Lund studies in geography. Series B, Human geography ; $v number 44
490 1_ $a Magic treehouse series ; $v #9

A *series-like phrase* or a *series-like statement* is a phrase that appears on an item, which seems like maybe it could be a series, but it really is not. Often it is a phrase associated with a previously independent publishing house that has been bought out and is systematically put on hundreds of other manifestations.

If a cataloger looks at the authority record for the phrase in the LC Authorities website (http://authorities.loc.gov/) with the titles, the title authority record will indicate whether the phrase is considered a series. If it is, follow the instructions for series; and if it is not, the authority record will clarify whether the phrase should be included as a quoted note. Quoted notes are supplied in the 500 field.

Notes (RDA 1.10, etc.)

In RDA, the instructions in chapters 2 through 7 might specify that the cataloger create a note. What is a note? And where does it go in the bibliographic record?

Notes cover a lot of territory and, for this reason, are easier to think about in MARC. Notes are entered in the MARC 5XX field. Some information is specifically to be included in notes. Other information is put here if there is no other place in the record for it. The notes listed here are the most widely used ones, but there are others.

MARC 500 General Note

This is something of a catchall. It is used for quoted notes like the one for series-like phrases and notes that do not have another specific place to go. Check OCLC *Bibliographic Formats and Standards* (http://www.oclc.org/bibformats/en.html) or LC's MARC bibliographic (http://www.loc.gov/marc/bibliographic/) page for a comprehensive list of note fields. If none of them applies, then use the 500.

500 _ _ $a "A fireside book."
500 _ _ $a Title from DVD label.
500 _ _ $a Produced by the National Film Board of Canada, in cooperation with WGBH.
500 _ _ $a Originally produced for the PBS television series, Nova.
500 _ _ $a Based on: The block book / Elizabeth S. Hirsch, editor.
500 _ _ $a DVD version of a documentary produced in 2008 (c2009), with added features.
500 _ _ $a "An Apple paperback"—Cover.
500 _ _ $a "Second in the trilogy"—Cover.
500 _ _ $a Special features: "One year later" update (20 minutes); conversations with the director and producers (director/producer Paul Saltzman, producer Patricia Aquino) (22 minutes); deleted and extended scenes; stills gallery.

MARC 504 Bibliography, Etc. Note (RDA 7.16 Supplementary Content)

This note was described in the previous chapter under expression-level content since it houses the Supplementary Content (RDA 7.16).

MARC 505 Table of Contents Note (RDA 25.1 Related Work; RDA 7.22 Duration)

This should always be included for music recordings. For books, it should be included if the chapter titles would be helpful in a keyword search or if it is a compilation of papers, essays, short stories, poems, novels, and so on. If each part was authored by a different person, that information can also be included. For bonus materials on a DVD/Blu-ray, use a 500 note. The first indicator is usually 0, which will display "Contents" to the catalog users. Other possible first indicators are 1 (Incomplete contents) and 2 (Partial contents). The second indicator specifies whether the contents note is unenhanced or enhanced. An unenhanced contents note (second indicator blank) is only searchable by keyword and will have all of the information entered in subfield a. An enhanced contents note (second indicator of 0) allows the titles to be searched in a title search. The title will be in subfield t, authors (if applicable) are in subfield r, and miscellaneous information (numbering, duration) is in subfield g. Please note that the authors are not searchable in the author index.

> 505 0_ $a v. 1. The fellowship of the ring—v. 2. The two towers—v. 3. The return of the king.
>
> 505 2 0 $t Why not? A prelude—$t Nothing happened—$t Good for nothing—$t Nothing takes center stage—$t Nothing becomes center stage.
>
> 505 0 0 $t Early in the morning / $r Paul Stookey $g (1:33)— $t 500 miles / $r Hedy West $g (2:46)— $t Sorrow / $r Stookey, Peter Yarrow $g (2:49)— $t This train / $r Yarrow, Stookey $g (2:03)— $t Bamboo / $r Van Ronk $g (2:25)— $t It's raining / $r Stookey, Yarrow $g (4:20)— $t If I had my way / $r Gary Davis $g (2:17)— $t Cruel war / $r Yarrow, Stookey $g (3:26)— $t Lemon tree / $r Will Holt $g (2:52)— $t If I had a hammer / $r Seeger, Hayes $g (2:06)— $t Autumn to May / $r Yarrow, Stookey $g (2:43)— $t Where have all the flowers gone / $r Seeger $g (3:54).

MARC 508 Creation/Production Credits Note (RDA 7.24 Artistic and/or Technical Credit) and 511 Participant or Performer Note (RDA 7.23 Performer, Narrator, and/or Presenter)

These were discussed in the previous chapter under expression-level content.

MARC 515 Numbering Peculiarities Note (RDA 2.17.5 Note on Numbering of Serials)

This is used for serials when the publishers did something unexpected. Examples are the skipping of some numbers, numbering two issues the same, or some issues not published.

> 515 _ _ $a Issues for March 1988 and January 1989 both numbered 21.
>
> 515 _ _ $a Numbering varies; some issues have dates only.

MARC 518 Date/Time and Place of an Event Note (RDA 7.11.2 Place of Capture; RDA 7.11.3 Date of Capture)

Mostly used for music CDs and occasionally DVDs to note when they were recorded. Only use if the information is present on the item.

518 _ _ $a Recorded in March 1983 at Momaday's home in Tucson, Ariz.
518 _ _ $a Taped off-air with permission in October 2002.

MARC 520 Summary Note (RDA 7.10 Summarization of the Content (Core Element for LC/PCC[8])

The summary note should be used for all fiction juvenile materials and for all DVDs. Use for nonfiction juvenile materials if the table of contents does not adequately convey the topic or if there is no table of contents. As noted in Chapter 3, summaries have not historically been given for adult books, but they are becoming more common. For fictional items, make sure the summary does not give away the ending. It is okay to use sentence fragments. If you are using the blurb directly from the item or a website for the item, either remove the superlatives and subjective statements or note where the blurb came from, so that it does not look like the library is making those statements.

520 _ _ $a Mama Bear hopes to teach the cubs to think of others instead of only themselves by having them help an elderly neighbor clean out her attic.
520 _ _ $a Presents the history of women's suffrage in the United States through the dramatic, often turbulent friendship of Elizabeth Cady Stanton and Susan B. Anthony. Part 1 covers the years from their youth up to the establishment of the National Woman Suffrage Association in 1868. Part 2 spans the period from 1868 to the passage in 1919 of the 19th amendment to the Constitution which gave women the vote.

MARC 521 Audience Note (RDA 7.7 Intended Audience [Core Element for LC[9]])

Use a MARC 521 audience note if information about the audience level is on the item or comes from an official website (like Accelerated Reader or Lexile). Do not make up this information yourself. For juvenile materials, this information can be reading level, interest grade, or interest age. It is rarely used for adult materials, unless it is for a specific audience. Make sure to be clear in your coding if you are conveying age or grade level (fourth grade is very different from 4 years old) and if the item is for a grade level or for a teacher of that grade level. For DVDs, the MPAA rating will be put here.

521 _ _ $a Teachers of grades 3–4.
521 0_ $a 3.1.
521 1_ $a 4–7.
521 2_ $a 7 and up.
521 8_ $a MPAA rating: PG-13; for extended sequences of intense fantasy action violence, and frightening images.
521 8_ $a Rating: TV 14.

MARC 525 Supplement (RDA 25.1 Related Work)

For use if a serial publication has had a supplement issued.

525 _ _ $a Supplement accompanies 29.

MARC 538 System Details Note (RDA 3.16.9 Special Playback Characteristic; 3.18 Video Characteristic; 3.19.3 Encoding Format; 3.19.5 Resolution; 3.19.6 Regional Encoding; 3.19.7 Encoded Bitrate; 3.20 Equipment or System Requirement)

For DVDs/Blu-ray, this includes region, definition, and screen ratio. For CD/DVD-ROMs, this is where you would put the system requirements needed to play the disc. Some of the information found here can also be put in the 340 and 344–347 fields. These are new fields that have recently been introduced to accommodate RDA. As their usage becomes more widespread, the 538 will no longer be used for the information that can be put elsewhere. Most of these fields are filled in from lists given in RDA.

538 _ _ $a DVD.
538 _ _ $a DVD, NTSC region 1, widescreen presentation; 5.1 surround, 2.0 stereo.
   OR
340 _ _ $b 4 3/4 in. $2 rda
344 _ _ $a digital $b optical $g surround $h Dolby Digital 5.1 $2 rda
344 _ _ $a digital $b optical $g stereo $h Dolby Digital 2.0 $2 rda
346 _ _ $b NTSC $2 rda
347 _ _ $a video file $b DVD video $e region 1 $2 rda

538 _ _ $a System requirements: Windows XP, Vista, or Windows 7; Adobe Acrobat Reader.

MARC 588 Source of Description Note (RDA 2.17.13 Note on Issue, Part, or Iteration Used as the Basis for Identification of the Resource)

Use for ebooks, often to indicate that the print version record was used as a template and then a few changes were made. Also use for serials to indicate which issue you used as the basis for the record.

588 _ _ $a Description based on print record version.
588 _ _ $a Description based on: No. 1 (June 1902); title from cover.

Identifier for the Manifestation (RDA 2.15.1) (Core)

Identifiers can be a numeric or alphanumeric string that is unique to a particular manifestation. Please note that although it is supposed to be unique, publishers can print previously used identifiers either by mistake or on purpose.

The most common identifier for books is the ISBN [International Standard Book Number] (MARC 020). New books have a 13-digit code. Older items will have a 10-digit code, and really old items will have a nine-digit code. Record the ISBN without dashes. You will need to add a leading zero to nine-digit codes. Newer DVDs and CDs may have an ISBN. The section on Qualification (RDA 2.15.1.7) tells us that it is possible to record a qualifier to distinguish if there are more than one identifiers of the same type or if it is important for identification.

020 _ _ $a 9781567932478 $q (pbk.)
020 _ _ $a 978140005218X $q (paperback)

Serials have an ISSN (International Standard Serial Number). These are an eight-digit code and are recorded in MARC 022. Leave the dash in.

022 0_ $a 0886–4950

DVDs/Blu-rays and CDs often have a UPC code and are recorded in a MARC 024 field. The UPC is the number printed below an item's barcode. While patrons may not be likely to look this number up, it is very helpful to other catalogers in determining if a bibliographic record matches the item in hand.

024 1 _ $a 078073004997

For all disc items, there may be a publisher-assigned number that appears on the disc. These go in field 028. See previously given sources for further information on coding and formatting.

DVD
028 40 $a 88589 $b PBS Home Video
028 40 $a 43648-K $b Films for the Humanities & Sciences

CD
028 02 $a STMA 8007 $b Tamla Motown
028 02 $a H-71260 $b Nonesuch Records

ITEM-LEVEL CONTENT

Item-level content records information about the specific copy/copies owned by a particular library. The item record has the call number, barcode, and availability information. It can also include myriad internal information, including notation of multiple parts (book with a disc), who cataloged it and when, number of checkouts, and so on.

Item-level records also include information that only pertains to this particular copy, like missing pages or being signed by the author.

MARC FIXED FIELD CONTENT (AKA CONTROL FIELDS)

Depending on the integrated library system (ILS) in use, the cataloger may have more or fewer fixed fields to complete. This is because each system can choose to break them out differently. Here, we describe some of the highly encoded fields related to RDA; additional control fields can be explored through MARC documentation found online.

Remember, these are highly encoded fields that will likely be filled in by the cataloger typing just a few characters, choosing from a drop-down menu, and so on. Examples of these fields filled out according to RDA are available in the RDA record section of Appendix A of this book.

Leader/06 Type of Record

This field dictates which other control fields will appear. For books, ebooks, and serials, encode this "a." For CDs, encode "i" for audiobooks and "j" for music. DVDs and Blu-ray are encoded "k."

Leader/07 Bibliographic Level

For most items, the bibliographic level will be "m" for monograph. Serials are "s."

Leader/18 Descriptive Cataloging Form

This field is where catalogers indicate the content standard used in cataloging. For RDA, enter "i." The 040 will also have $e rda added by the cataloger.

Leader/19 Multipart Resource Record Level

This will not be used with non-serial library materials like books, DVDs, or CDs.

007/00 Physical Description Fixed Field—Category of Material

The category of material you are cataloging (book, ebook, music, movie, etc.) will determine how the rest of the 007 is coded. Textual items are encoded "t," sound recordings are encoded "s," and video recordings are encoded "v."

008/35–37 Fixed-Length Data Elements—Language

Three-letter codes for the language of materials can be found in the MARC Code List for Languages (http://www.loc.gov/marc/languages/). This fixed field's content is used by patrons when limiting a search to materials in a certain language.

CONCLUSION

In this section, we provided a nuts-and-bolts approach to cataloging manifestations and items in MARC. Going through cataloging in MARC-number order, we described how RDA instructions are interpreted and applied, and gave examples. We also briefly explained how some of the control fields in MARC records are filled in.

No one is expected to learn all of this by heart, but knowing where this information is and being able to come back to it when necessary is a cataloger's greatest strength.

Your work in cataloging with RDA is not done here, however, since you still need to account for the intellectual contents of the materials being cataloged. In the next chapters, we describe how that work is carried out through the creation of subject headings and call numbers.

NOTES

1. Variant Title. Glossary. RDA Toolkit. http://access.rdatoolkit.org/ (Accessed February 28, 2015)
2. RDA 2.8: "Place of publication, publisher's name, and date of publication are core elements for published resources. Other sub-elements of publication statements are optional."
3. Copyright Date. Glossary. RDA Toolkit. http://access.rdatoolkit.org/ (Accessed February 28, 2015)
4. RDA 2.11 "Copyright date is a core element if neither the date of publication nor the date of distribution is identified."
5. See LC-PCC PS for 7.17.1.3.
6. See LC-PCC PS for 3.5.1.4.4.
7. RDA 2.6: "Core elements are numeric and/or alphabetic designation of first issue or part of sequence, chronological designation of first issue or part of sequence, numeric and/or alphabetic designation of last issue or part of sequence, and chronological designation of last issue or part of sequence. Other numbering is optional."
8. LC-PCC PS for 7.10: "Summarization of the content is a core element for LC for fiction intended for children."
9. LC-PCC PS for 7.7: "Intended audience is a core element for LC for resources intended for children."

SUGGESTED RESOURCE

OCLC. 2015. *Bibliographic Formats and Standards* http://www.oclc.org/bibformats/en.html Library of Congress. n.d. MARC Bibliographic. http://www.loc.gov/marc/bibliographic/

CHAPTER 7

Access Points for Names

This chapter is about access points for creators and ones for titles. In the past, *access points* were often printed at the top left-hand side of each card catalog card, and the cards were alphabetized in the drawer based on these access points. They truly were *points of access* into the catalog, and the three common ones were title, author, and subject (we discuss subjects in the next chapter). Access points were separate from the main guts of the cataloging record (and there was only one per card)—they were something additional, a way to find the catalog card, which in turn provided a way to access the resource.

In the MARC environment, as many access points as needed for creators and titles get added to cataloging records along with the description and subject headings. With keyword searching, you can use just about any character string in a record as a point of access—primarily because it can be searchable. We formulate access points according to RDA (described below) as a way of allowing consistent access to resources for patrons. Charles Cutter envisioned a catalog where it was possible to collocate by name, title, or subject.[1] Without access points, it would be virtually impossible to pull *all* of the records for related items. Imagine trying to find all the items by a prolific author who changed her name in the middle of her career if the only searchable elements were the way her name was written on the title page. It would be nearly impossible to find everything the library had of hers. With an identical access point for the author included in each and every cataloging record, however, collocating all of her works suddenly becomes much easier.

Access points for creators and titles are always based on the descriptive guts of the catalog record and are formulated to provide necessary information from the outset. The main feature of access points is that they allow for collocation of results—so that all of a person's opus held in a given library will be retrieved through a search of a single character string. Let us see how that might play out in the real world.

Access Points in Action

Earlier we gave the classic example of an author who has changed names over the course of her career. To provide access to the author's entire body of work, a single character string will be used as an access points in all of the bibliographic records—in addition to the description that RDA requires. Adding an authorized access point will allow end users to do a comprehensive search on the author using either name.

RDA INSTRUCTIONS

RDA provides instructions for catalogers on how to create access points for what is referred to as PFC (persons, families, and corporate bodies) and searchable titles. At present, RDA does not provide instructions about subject access, but there are placeholder chapters that will provide this information in the future. In this *Crash Course,* we focus on the high points for creating and using access points for persons, corporate bodies, series, and preferred titles for works. We do this because, in our experience, these are the most common access points catalogers see and use.

RDA describes how to create the basic cataloging record. Once that is done, the cataloger must determine whether access points are required to better describe and/or make the resource findable. If access points are created, a related question is how they should be encoded in MARC (a topic not addressed in RDA).

In this chapter, we give examples of situations when access points should be created and show you how they look. If you have any doubt about whether an access point should be created or not for a given resource, you should always look for instructions in the RDA Toolkit, especially in the sections that cover relationships.

Collaborative Access Point Creation

RDA gives us instructions for creating access points—theoretically then, every cataloger approaching the creation of an access point for a certain person would create the same access point in the same way. The fact of the matter is, though, creating an access point can take a bit of work (called *authority work*). Theoretically, different sources could be consulted and different conclusions about how the access point should look could be drawn.

Rather than to test the idea that everyone would create the same access point if given a chance, catalogers prefer to have one highly trained cataloger formulate the access point *once* and then share the results of that work with everyone else. It is not surprising that the cataloging community makes a concerted effort to share formulations for access points—it already strives to share cataloging records!

When you catalog, rather than to reinvent the wheel each time you are faced with supplying an access point for a person (or, as we will later see, for a corporate body or series or work), it is best to first look to see if someone has already created an *authority record* for that person in the shared databases that are available.

Authority Records

An *authority record* is a combination of a few different things, all to help catalogers with their work (patrons generally do not even see the authority records). First, the authority record features the authorized form of the access point. This is the form that a highly trained cataloger created and that, subsequently, all catalogers can use in their bibliographic records.

Authority records can also include:

• Phrasings that reasonably *could* be the access point, but that are not for some reason or another (maybe they were based on the previous name, were created under different rules, are written in a foreign language or use a foreign script, etc.). These are considered "Use for" terms and will never appear in bibliographic records as access points. The integrated library system (ILS), however, will use these "use for" terms to redirect patrons to the authorized form of the access point (see Figure 7.1).

• Information about the entity being described. For example, in authority records for people, it is possible to include information about that person's gender, affiliations, profession, and languages.

• Sources for the information recorded in the authority record. Wikipedia, emails from authors to catalogers, titles of books by an author, and so on can all be sources.

• Pseudonyms for individuals with more than one identity that will serve as cross-references to the authorized form of the access point in the ILS.

• Information about when the record was created, whether it has been updated recently, and, at times, instructions for its use.

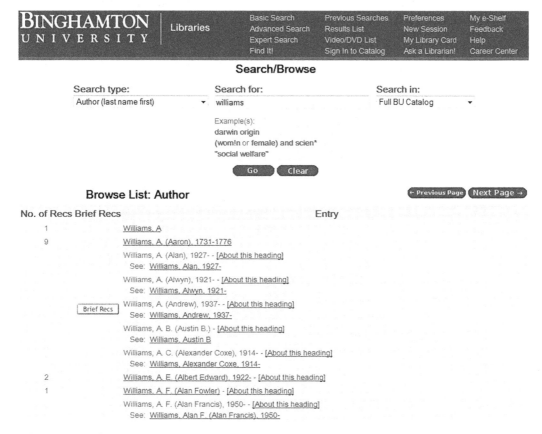

Figure 7.1   Results of an Author Name Search.

Authority records are, perhaps unsurprisingly, marked up using MARC. They are also encoded to be integrated with linked data on the semantic web.

NACO

The Name Authority Cooperative Program (NACO, pronounced *nay-co*) is run by the Program for Cooperative Cataloging (PCC) at LC. NACO participants help LC add authority records for personal names, corporate names, jurisdictional names, preferred (uniform) titles, and series to the Name Authority File (NAF). NACO participants (i.e., librarians) must attend extensive training and maintain a certain level of contribution. Usually, an institution is the NACO member with multiple trained staff, although in some cases individual membership is allowed.

NACO is not the only program the PCC sponsors. Other PCC programs are Monographic Bibliographic Record Cooperative Program (BIBCO), Cooperative Online Serials Program (CONSER), and Subject Authority Cooperative Program (SACO).[2]

Authority Files: LC Authorities

Authority records are kept together in a searchable database called an *authority file*. Authority files are available electronically and are kept on a national level, and can also be kept on a consortial level. They can also be maintained on a local level in the library's ILS. International authority records from a variety of national authority files are available through OCLC's Virtual International Authority File (VIAF) (pronounced *vee-off*) (http:// viaf.org/). VIAF is currently an international aggregator of authority records; it is expected to function as a true international authority file in the future.

For your cataloging, you will want to consult the U.S. national authority file in search of authority records for the people, corporate bodies, series, and works that relate to your materials. The LC Authorities website (http://authorities.loc.gov/) allows catalogers to search for access points for subjects (i.e., subject headings, which we will discuss in the next chapters), names (for persons and for corporate bodies), titles (including titles for series), and name/title access points that provide access to works through the name of the author or creator.

The LC Authorities website offers free access to all of the authority records housed at LC. Detailed help screens guide new users, and from the main search area, search tips are clearly visible. For example, with subject, name, title, name/title searches, the searches are all left-anchored, and truncation is automatic. This is a great place to search, for example, if someone has already created an authorized access point for Andrew Williams, the bass player on the music CD you are cataloging.

This LC Authorities website does have its limitations, however. First, it can be difficult for the uninitiated because of the way the results are displayed; it is not always clear that opening and reading the authority record is necessary, but it is (see Sidebar 7.1)! LC authority records in the authority file tend to be based on published print resources that LC has cataloged. Patrons local to your area who donate self-published books to your library will probably not be represented in LC's authority file. We will talk more about how to create an access point yourself in the next section.

SIDEBAR 7.1   PRO TIP: USING THE LC AUTHORITIES WEBSITE

When using access points found in the Library of Congress Authorities website, it is important to open the authority record and take a look at it instead of just selecting from the results screen. Why? You will find additional instructions in the authority record that may even tell you not to use the access point! LC authority records are encoded in MARC, but can be viewed in a user-friendly format by catalogers who prefer to save their MARC–viewing for bibliographic records. To switch from the MARC display, click the Labelled Display tab at the top of the record.

AUTHORITY CONTROL AND AUTHORITY VENDORS

Authority control is the process of making sure access points in bibliographic records match the authorized form in an authority record. Part of this process is done at the time of cataloging. However, some of the process is done later. Authority vendors provide a service that allows authority control to be an automated process. At a set time (weekly, monthly, quarterly) a vendor will pull all the new bibliographic records that have been added to an institution's catalog since the last processing. They will then check the access points on these records to see what new authority records need to be added to the local authority file and to see if the access points match an existing authority record. If possible, some changes and corrections will be made automatically. If the change is not one that can be made by the computer, a report will be generated for the cataloger to look at later. The vendor will also provide updated versions of authority records an institution already has and let the institution know what authority records should be deleted.

Making Access Points for Your Bibliographic Records

Most of the materials you will receive will not involve the creation of new access points—access points will already exist because an authority record will have been created and uploaded to the Name Authority File (NAF). It is usually just a matter of searching for the authority record and then using the authorized form of the access point in the catalog record.

If, however, there is no authority record for a person and you are required to make up the access point, never fear! The flowchart at Figure 7.2 will guide you through the thought process involved in providing access for creators in bibliographic records.

Because personal name access points are some of the more common kinds of access points you will be required to provide in cataloging, we will begin by describing those. After that, we will talk about corporate body access points. Finally, we will turn our attention to access points that include titles or elements of titles, specifically series access points and work access points.

Personal Names: Principles and Features

If you are cataloging and there is no authority record for an individual who should be included in the bibliographic record, you will need to create an access point yourself.

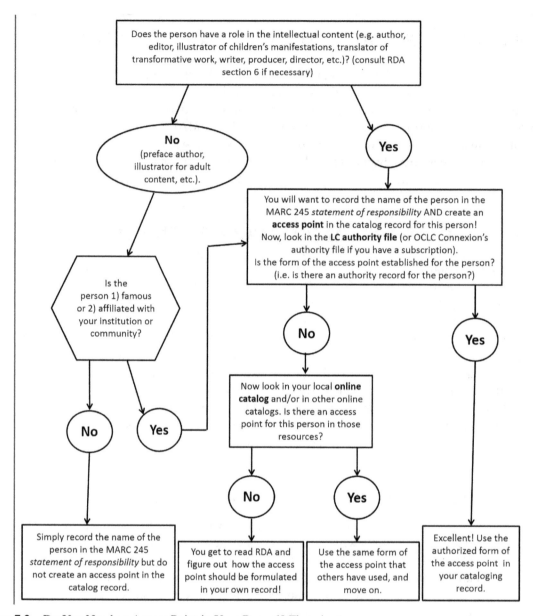

Figure 7.2 Do You Need an Access Point in Your Record? Flowchart.

As you may expect, personal names are names for people. RDA's chapter 8 is "General Guidelines on Recording Attributes of Persons, Families, and Corporate Bodies"; it supports the instructions in RDA's chapter 9, "Identifying Persons." We focus on RDA chapter 9 in this section.

People's names appear in access points based on how they want to be known: RDA instructs catalogers to use the "preferred name" or the "the name by which the person is most commonly known." If an author's name appears on the title page of her first book as Debbie Watson-Jones, the cataloger will base the access point on the name as it appears. The cataloger will not wonder if Debbie's full name is Deborah or if Jones is her legal married name. Instead, the cataloger will apply the RDA rules in chapter 9 and create the access points based on the way the name is presented.

Sometimes a single person will sign his name differently on different items. The inclusion or exclusion of a middle name or middle initial is an example. How much is there is a question of *fullness*. Fullness is addressed in 9.2.2.5.1, where RDA states "choose as the preferred name the form most commonly found." If the cataloger creating the access point searches for an author online and realizes that he has already published (or self-published, or just signed in some way) two books with his first, middle, and last names and one book with just his first name, the access point will include all three since that is more commonly found. A related question about Change of Name is addressed in 9.2.2.7, where RDA tells us, "If a person has changed his or her name, choose the latest name or form of name as the preferred name." In this case, if faced with two versions of the person's name, the cataloger will choose the more recent. Finally, the question of how to record the hyphenated last name is addressed in RDA 9.2.2.10 Compound Surnames where RDA explains, "Treat a surname as a compound surname if it consists of two or more proper names separated by either a space or a hyphen."[3]

CREATING UNIQUE ACCESS POINTS

Another of the main principles associated with access points is that each and every one should be unique and specific. For people in the bibliographic universe with names like Robert Smith, catalogers have to work hard to differentiate the character strings.

Why differentiate? Traditionally, catalogers have not wanted the same character string to represent more than one person. This is not the philosophy that Amazon or other online retailers use, but then again, they are not information professionals the way librarians are. RDA unequivocally guides catalogers in this matter by stating that one of its principles is "Differentiation." Differentiation is as important for resources (one book should not be confused with another, for example) as it is for people and other entities involved in the creation of a resource. RDA 0.4.3.1 words it this way: "The data describing a resource should differentiate that resource from other resources. The data describing an entity associated with a resource should differentiate that entity from other entities, and from other identities used by the same entity."[4]

In the past, it was possible to have undifferentiated name headings—where multiple authors would be designated by the same access point. Jones, Sally today should only represent one individual, not multiple ones. Why? First, regardless of the character string(s) assigned at birth to authors, it should be possible for users to collocate all of the library's holdings written by an individual. This can only happen if people with identical names have access points that are differentiated, or that include information other than just their names. Additionally, future plans to add library data to the linked data web will require all individuals to have their own unique access point.

RDA guides catalogers in the creation of access points that are relevant to the resources being cataloged. Some elements of the access points are core in RDA, meaning that they are required. Others are required if needed to differentiate the access points for two different authors. For many of these, LC and PCC elected to add information to access points if that information is known. This means that some information might be added to break a conflict, while at other times, information might be added simply in anticipation of preventing future conflicts. In this way, catalogers are cultivating a system of foresight. Table 7.1 gives information about the kind of elements potentially included in an access point, the associated instructions by number, and notes from RDA as to whether it is core or not.

Table 7.1   Core Elements for Personal Name Access Points[5]

RDA instructions		Notes
9.2	Name of the Person	Preferred name for the person is a core element.
9.2.2	Preferred Name for the Person	CORE ELEMENT
9.3	Date Associated with the Person	Date of birth and date of death are core elements. Period of activity of the person is a core element only when needed to distinguish a person from another person with the same name.
9.4	Title of the Person	Title of the person is a core element when it is a word or phrase indicative of royalty, nobility, or ecclesiastical rank or office, or a term of address for a person of religious vocation. Any other term indicative of rank, honour, or office is a core element when needed to distinguish a person from another person with the same name.
9.5	Fuller Form of Name	A fuller form of name is a core element when needed to distinguish a person from another person with the same name.
9.6	Other Designation Associated with the Person	Other designation associated with the person is a core element for a Christian saint, a spirit, a person named in a sacred scripture or an apocryphal book, a fictitious or legendary person, or a real non-human entity. For other persons, other designation associated with the person is a core element when needed to distinguish a person from another person with the same name.

Building an Access Point for a Personal Name

Personal name access points generally start with the same basic elements. When cataloging, begin with the person's last name, follow it with a comma, and then include the person's first name and middle name(s) or initials if that is how the person prefers to be known. Some people, including pop stars, clergy, and royalty, may choose not to use a last name. RDA has instructions to guide the cataloger in these cases among the instructions included at 9.2.2 Preferred Name for the Person. Since these cases are so rare, however, you will likely never have to make an access point for a person that does not begin with a last name.

If you cannot find an authority record and if you are not a member of NACO, it is okay to stop at this point and not add anything further to the name. This access point will be used in your local system, and 99.9% of the time, it will be unique. You are not required to do research into the person and make a unique access point locally. The following information will help you understand already established authorized access points and why different elements were chosen.

Often dates of birth are known by the cataloger, especially since the dates of birth appear on the copyright application forms submitted to LC. These dates are core, and, according to RDA, should be added as part of the access point—they also can differentiate between two people with otherwise identical first and last names. RDA 9.3.4 Period of Activity of the Person, "a date or range of dates indicative of the period in which a person was active in his or her primary field of endeavour," is a core element.

Figure 7.3   RDA Training, Part 10: Eschewing Cataloger's Bias.

Sometimes dates are not enough to differentiate between two people's access points in the national authority file. Some people prefer to provide initials instead of spelling out the fullest form of their names. An example is librarian Edward Michael Corrado who always signs his name Edward M. Corrado. If there were two Edward M. Corrados, that would be a conflict. Catalogers can break a conflict by adding, in parentheses, the spelled-out form of the abbreviated name. This is explained under the Fuller Form of Name instructions in RDA 9.5, and practice is that if a cataloger knows the qualifier, it is possible to add it to the access point.

If it is still not possible to differentiate between two different persons—if dates of birth or death, if fuller form of the name, and if Period of Activity of the Person are not enough (see RDA 9.6.1.9), catalogers will turn to RDA 9.16 for help supplying information about the person's Profession or Occupation or RDA 9.4.1.9, Other Term of Rank, Honour, or Office. If discovered, that information can be added to the access point as well. This information goes in parentheses, and tends to be titles (such as honorifics) and other words associated with a person.

See Figure 7.3 for an example of what not to include in the access point when differentiating persons under RDA.

Personal Name Access Points in MARC

A lot of RDA instructions and glimpses at practice were given earlier. Here, we provide some nuts-and-bolts examples that have been encoded in MARC.

When creating a bibliographic record, the first-named author or creator will be encoded with a three-digit MARC code beginning with the number 1. Catalogers tend to refer to this as being included in the "1XX" (pronounced *one ex ex*). You will recall from the MARC chapter that there are some mnemonics associated with MARC, and in this case, the first author of a book will always appear in the catalog record with a number beginning with the digit 1. For example, personal name access points will be encoded in the 100 for authors or creators who are individuals. The first indicator is almost always a 1 (it will be 0 for historical figures and royalty who do not have surnames [i.e., last names]). The second indicator is blank. The name portion will be in $a and dates are in $d. Qualifiers (spelling out the name) are in $q and other information (title, profession, etc.) goes in $c. These indicators and subfields are the same regardless if the name appears in a 100, 600, 700, or 800 field.

For his book *Cardiac Drugs in Pregnancy,* Professor John Anthony's access point in the 100 will look like this:

100 1 _ $a Anthony, John $c (Professor of obstetrics and gynecology)

Anthony Keasbey is identified with birth and death dates, but also has the qualifier for his middle name as part of his access point. For his 1882 book, his name will appear in the bibliographic record in the 100 as the following:

100 1 _ $a Keasbey, Anthony Q. $q (Anthony Quinton), $d 1824–1895.

Each catalog record only has one 1XX field. If there is an additional author (or two, or more, potentially), their access points will be added as 700s. Additionally, if an individual is associated with the expression (e.g. an illustrator of children's materials or a writer of added commentary (see RDA 20.2 Contributor) and is important enough to be included as an access point, the access points for those persons will be entered as700s.

700 1_ $a Bellinger, Carl-Hermann, 1935– $e writer of added commentary.

Only authors or creators are placed in the 100 Main Entry—Personal Name. Editors are always encoded in the 700 since they are not authors or creators For an edited volume with five editors, only the first editor is required in the 700 Added Entry—Personal Name.. According to the MARC documentation, the 700 field is repeatable. In this scenario, therefore, the other four editors can be included in 700 fields (one for each author) if the cataloger wishes. Since this volume has no author, there is no 100 in the record for this book.

245 00 $a Reading at a crossroad? : $b disjunctures and continuities in conceptions and practices of reading in the 21st century / $c edited by Rand J. Spiro, Michael Deschryver, Michelle Schira Hagerman, Paul Morsink, and Penny Thompson.

700 1_ $a Spiro, Rand J., $e editor.

Relationship Designators (RDA 29.1.5) (i.e., Relator Terms)

Relationship Designators (RDA 29.1.5), also called relator terms, clarify the role of the person (or corporate body) indicated in the access point to the material being catalogued. What does this mean? If a person is an author, catalogers include the relator term for author at the end of the access point like so:

100 1 Agunias, Dovelyn Rannveig, $e author.
700 1 Newland, Kathleen, $e author. (Program for Cooperative Cataloging 2013)

Relationship designators are listed in Appendix I of RDA. Some common relationship designators enumerated in RDA I.2 and I.3 (with their definitions) include the following:

RDA I.2.1 Relationship Designators for Creators (Work-level relationships)	RDA I.3.1 Relationship Designators for Contributors (Expression-level relationships)	RDA I.2.2 Relationship Designators for Other Persons, Families, or Corporate Bodies Associated with a Work
author	abridger	director
librettist	arranger of music	host institution
screenwriter	costume designer	issuing body
compiler	editor	producer
composer	illustrator	
interviewee	performer	
interviewer	translator	
photographer	writer of supplementary textual content	
	writer of introduction	
	writer of preface	

These lists are not complete! They do, however, give an idea of the kinds of Relationship Designators put forth in RDA.

Although RDA does not require the use of relationship designators, Program for Cooperative Cataloging (PCC) catalogers are required to add these relator terms in the MARC 100 and 700 fields.[6] The MARC $4 relator codes are not necessary if a $e relationship designator is provided. $4 works the same as $e, but uses a three-letter code instead of a term. Before the introduction of RDA, $4 was often used for music and occasionally for DVDs.

Other PCC guidelines include the use of the most specific term (in their example, they explain that a librettist is specific kind of author, so $e librettist is preferred to $e author). Finally, if a single person has more than one role in the creation of the material, it is possible to add more than one $e relationship designator—these additions will be in work, expression, manifestation, item (WEMI) order, as they are listed in RDA. PCC gives us the following example:

100 1_ $a Stone, Melicent, $e author, $e illustrator.[7]

Here, $e author is a relationship designator for a creator of the work, and $e illustrator is a relationship designator for a contributor associated with an expression. In WEMI order, the work precedes the expression, and authors are associated with works; illustrators with the expression. This means that the author relationship precedes the illustrator relationship in the cataloging record since work-level involvement precedes expression-level involvement.

Relator terms are, at first blush, deceptively similar to the $c (Titles and other words associated with a name) that can be part of an authorized access point for a person's name. The main difference is that $c (Titles and other words associated with a name) are permanent parts of a person's access point, provided to differentiate between two people with otherwise identical names.

Relationship designators help clarify a person's (or a corporate body's) *relationship* to the material being cataloged, so they might change from resource to resource. Returning to the example of librarian Edward M. Corrado, he is the first author of one resource and an editor of another. In the cataloging record for the book where he is first author, his access point will appear in the 100 field followed by $e author. In the record for the resource where he is editor, the access point for his name will appear in the 700 field followed by $e editor.

Corporate Bodies: Principles and Features

Persons can be responsible for the creation of intellectual content, but in many cases, so are corporate bodies.

What are *corporate bodies*? RDA defines them as "an organization or group of persons and/or organizations that is identified by a particular name and that acts, or may act, as a unit."[8] Corporate bodies can be corporations or other businesses, schools, nonprofits, musical groups, 4-H groups, Boy Scout troops, political groups, governmental bodies, and so on. They will normally be entered in MARC records as 110 Main Entry—Corporate Name fields if they function as the primary author or creator. The second author or creator associated with the expression would be entered in the 710 Added Entry—Corporate Name field.

Corporate bodies can also be meetings or events such as a world's fair, a conference, a Super Bowl, or an art exhibition. In cataloging records, meeting names will be entered in the 111 or the 711 if they are related to the creation of the work or the expression.

Table 7.2   Core Elements of Corporate Body Names in RDA[9]

RDA Instructions		Notes
11.2	Name of the Corporate Body	Preferred name for the corporate body is a core element.
11.2.2	Preferred Name for the Corporate Body	CORE ELEMENT

Just as there were instructions for creating access points for persons, there are instructions in RDA for creating access points for corporate bodies. Recall that RDA chapter 8 is "General Guidelines on Recording Attributes of Persons, Families, and Corporate Bodies"; RDA chapter 8 also supports the instructions in RDA chapter 11, "Identifying Corporate Bodies." In this *Crash Course,* we discuss two main kinds of corporate bodies requiring slightly different approaches in the creation of the access point.

Again, you will likely not have to create many access points from scratch, but it helps understand how they were constructed no matter who was behind it. In the following section, we focus on RDA chapter 11's instructions.

Table 7.2 shows the parts of the access point that are core in RDA.

Corporate Body Names Entered in Direct Order and MARC

Per RDA 11.2.2.4, to create an access point, the cataloger will "record the name of a corporate body as it appears in resources associated with the body."[10] Many access points for corporate bodies list the name in *direct order*. The first word of an access point for a name in direct order is the first word of the corporate body's name. For example,

Nine Inch Nails (Musical group)

In the above example, the name does not intuitively represent a corporate body. Musical group is added in parentheses because the name does not sound like a musical group otherwise. RDA 11.7.1.4 instructs us to add the Type of Corporate Body to the preferred name in this case. Other examples given include Spacecraft, Program, Fraternal order, Firm, Church, Radio station, and Television station. Terms Indicating Incorporation and Certain Other Terms (RDA 11.2.2.10) gives instructions for adding (Incorporated) and others as necessary to access points. In a MARC cataloging record for a compact disc by the group, the MARC looks like this:

110 2_ $a Nine Inch Nails (Musical group)

The 110 Main Entry—Corporate Name field is used for the corporate body responsible for the work. The first indicator is 2, meaning that the name is in direct order. Again, this simply means that the first word of the access point is the first word of the corporate body's name. Important to note: initial articles (i.e., *the, a, an* in English) are omitted in the authorized form of names that start with one. For example, *The New York Times* is authorized as 110 2 _ $a New York Times Company.

Subordinate and Related Bodies Recorded Subordinately (RDA 11.2.2.14) and MARC

Not all corporate body names are entered in direct order in the access point. This second situation generally occurs when a corporate body's name is so generic that it must be preceded by a location (jurisdiction name) or some other name of a bigger entity with which it is affiliated. RDA refers to these as Subordinate and Related Bodies Recorded Subordinately (RDA 11.2.2.14). The first indicator is a 1, meaning that the name is a juris-diction name. In most instances, one or more $b's will be added following the jurisdiction name in $a, specifying a particular subordinate unit of the jurisdiction. An example is the Senate of the United States. It is a Legislative Body (RDA 11.2.2.14.9). The Senate is part of the U.S. Congress, but lots of countries have congresses, so the corporate body name "Congress" is not terribly precise.

Here is the 1XX field for the U.S. Senate's Committee on Agriculture, Nutrition, and Forestry, the author of these legislative hearings (the title of which is given in the 245).

110 1_ $a United States. $b Congress. $b Senate. $b Committee on Agriculture, Nu-trition, and Forestry, $e author.

245 10 $a Drought, fire, and freeze : $b the economics of disasters for America's agricultural producers : hearing before the Committee on Agriculture, Nutrition and Forestry, United States Senate, One Hundred Thirteenth Congress, first ses-sion, February 14, 2013.

Remember, this is a corporate body for which we are creating an access point, but that access point happens to begin with a geographic location. This is not an access point for the country, but for the corporate body!

Titles as Access Points

Titles can also serve as access points. This makes sense because patrons may want to search for a resource based on the title. That title may be the title of the item, but in some instances, it might be the title of the series or even the name of an individual along with the title that could be searched.

Series Titles

It is important to transcribe series information, especially from books. There are actually two ways series information is recorded in MARC bibliographic records. First, it is transcribed as part of the description. Information about the volume and/or numbering is also included here. That entire transcription will go in the MARC 490 field. According to the way MARC is officially set up, this transcription will not be indexed with the titles, but it will be searchable as a keyword search and will display in the surrogate to help users understand whether the item meets their needs. The indicator shows whether or not the series is made into an access point. An indicator of 1 = make an access point. An indicator of 0 = do not make an access point.

The series name is transcribed as part of the manifestation information (discussed in Chapter 6).

490 1_ $a Lectures in advanced mathematics ; $v 1

As noted, however, descriptive information still needs to be formulated in order to create an access point.

To get the series title to appear in the title index, it needs to be added in a second field, the 8XX. If the authorized form of the series title's access point is just the name of the series, or perhaps if it includes some additional qualifiers at the end with further informa-tion about the series title, the access point for the series will be included in the 830 field of the bibliographic record. The 830 has a blank first indicator and second indicator of 0 (zero). This is because initial articles are never included in the authorized form of preferred titles. If there is volume numbering, it will go in $v.

830 _ 0 $a I can read it myself series.
830 _ 0 $a Best of Broadway ; $v v. 6.

If, for example, a series of books is written by the same person, then the series access point will begin with the authorized form of the access point for the person followed by the authorized form of the series title in a $t. All of this will be placed in an 800 field.

800 1_ $a Collins, Suzanne. $t Hunger Games ; $v bk. 2.

Preferred Titles for the Work (RDA 6.2.2)

The preferred title for the work "is the title or form of title chosen to identify the work" (RDA 6.2.2). This means that works originally written in other languages and translated, for example, into English, will have an additional access point in the bibliographic record for the preferred title of the work. Preferred titles also can be created for works published under different titles. RDA 6.2.2.4 gives the example of Johnathan Swift's *Gulliver's Travels,* which was first published under the title *Travels into Several Remote Nations of the World* and was signed by Lemuel Gulliver. Patrons may not expect to find the work they know as *Gulliver's Travels* under such a title. Similarly, pre-1500s works might be known under a variety of titles that could be spelled any number of ways. RDA 6.2.2.5 states that the preferred title for these follows the "form of title in the original language by which the work is identified in modern reference sources," meaning that *Beowulf*'s preferred title is Beowulf.

The addition of an access point for the preferred title is above and beyond the title and statement of responsibility that go in the 245 and that are transcribed from the title page (in this case, most likely in English). They are similar to access points for authors and creators in this way.

Preferred titles that have an author associated with them will go in a 240 Uniform Title field. Works without an author (anonymous, sacred scripture, etc.) will go in a 130 Main Entry—Uniform Title field. If you have a preferred title for something that is not the work itself (e.g., an anthology of many works, movie based on a book), the preferred title will go in 700 $t (700—Added Entry—Personal Name and $t Title of a work) if there is an author, or a 730 Added Entry—Uniform Title field if there is not. See LC's MARC Bibliographic site or OCLC's *Bibliographic Formats and Standards* for further explanation of the indicators and subfields for each of these.

240 10 $a Du côté de chez Swann. $l English
245 10 $a Swann's way / $c Marcel Proust ; translated with an introduction and notes by Lydia Davis ; general editor Christopher Prendergast.

There are also specific instructions in RDA about formulating preferred titles for special types of works—musical works (RDA 6.14.2); legal works (RDA 6.19.2); religious works (RDA 6.23.2); and official communications (RDA 6.26.2).

Conventional Collective Titles (MARC Name-Title Access Points)

Collective titles are defined in RDA as "a title proper that is an inclusive title for a resource containing several separately titled component parts. A collective title may be supplied by the publisher, etc., or devised by a cataloger."[11] In only a few situations is a collective title needed. While it is unlikely in most copy cataloging situations one would need to formulate such a title, a few examples are provided here so you know what they are when you see them (and understand why they should not be deleted).

240 10 $a Works.
240 10 $a Works. $k Selections
240 10 $a Essays.
240 10 $a Novels. $k Selections

These collective titles are used for collected or selected works of one author and are recorded in the 240 Uniform Title field of the bibliographic record. *Collected* in this case can either mean everything an author has ever written or everything an author has written in one format (novels, poetry, short stories, etc.). *Selected works* are just that, selections of one author's work that were previously published separately. An item that is a selection of Shakespeare's works would benefit from a collective title that could be searched in the catalog.

Collective titles are very rare, if not nonexistent, in A/V cataloging. In music, they are very common on scores, which are not covered in this book. They may be seen on music CDs where all the songs are by one composer. Generally the CDs will be of classical music, but could be for modern composers. Conventional collective titles are not used for CDs where the songs were composed by different people, even if only one person or group is the performer.

240 10 $a Songs. $k Selections
240 10 $a Motion picture music.
240 10 $a Concertos. $k Selections

CONCLUSION

In this chapter, we have gone through many of the considerations required for the creation of good access points. This is not everything, but this should be enough to get you started in understanding (1) what access points look like in MARC for persons, corporate bodies, and a number of kinds of titles; (2) the function of the authority file; and (3) what you need to know from RDA to get started in the case that you have to create them yourself.

NOTES

1. Charles Ammi Cutter. 1904. *Rules for a Dictionary Catalog.* Fourth edition, rewritten. Washington, D.C.: Government Printing Office. http://digital.library.unt.edu/ark:/67531/metadc1048/ (accessed February 26, 2015)
2. Program for Cooperative Cataloging. http://www.loc.gov/aba/pcc/ (accessed February 26, 2015)
3. See RDA 9.2.2 Preferred Name for the Person.
4. See RDA 0.4.3.1 Differentiation
5. Instructions taken from the RDA Toolkit, 2015. http://access.rdatoolkit.org/
6. The use of these relationship designators in cataloging records stems from a PCC policy that is available online: http://www.loc.gov/aba/pcc/rda/PCC%20RDA%20guidelines/Relat-Desig-Guidelines.docx

7. Program for Cooperative Cataloging. 2013. PCC Guidelines for the Application of Relationship Designators in Bibliographic Records. http://www.loc.gov/aba/pcc/rda/PCC%20RDA%20guidelines/Relat-Desig-Guidelines.docx

8. Corporate Body. 2015. RDA Toolkit, Glossary. http://access.rdatoolkit.org/

9. See RDA 11.2.2.4.

10. Instructions taken from the RDA Toolkit, 2015. http://access.rdatoolkit.org/

11. Collective Title. 2015. RDA Toolkit, Glossary. http://access.rdatoolkit.org/

CHAPTER 8

Subject Access
and Controlled Vocabularies

Subject access is complex, but it is an essential part of providing access to library materials. First in this chapter, we describe what subject access is. Then we talk about applying it in the creation of subject headings. Library of Congress Subject Headings (LCSH) and Sears List of Subject Headings (Sears) are two common examples. Finally, we talk about the genre headings that provide access to what an item is, not just to what it is about.

WHAT IS SUBJECT ACCESS?

Cataloging involves not only the descriptive work (in this case, creating description and access using RDA) but also subject access. In many ways, subject access is the quintessential part of cataloging that non-catalogers may associate with it. Three chapters have already been devoted to descriptive cataloging and to the access points based on the description. In this chapter, we focus on subject access (i.e., access to the intellectual content) of a resource; specifically on verbal (i.e., *word-based*) subject access.

Subject access plays out in two ways in library catalogs and on library shelves. The first is subject headings, the main topic of this chapter. Subject headings allow users to group together all of the items on a same topic as the results of the search. The second, classification, is the other way that subject access is permitted in the online catalog. Although the usefulness of call numbers in individual integrated library systems (ILSs) varies, call numbers are the way that items like books are organized on the shelves and they permit physical retrieval. Classification and call numbers are discussed in the next chapter.

As with the chapter focusing on access and access points, these chapters on subject access are quite meaty. We suggest that you read through them at least once, and then go back to focus more specifically on the parts that pertain to you and the cataloging task you have at hand when the time comes.

PROVIDING SUBJECT ACCESS

In the sections that follow this one, we will assume that the cataloger understands what an item is about, specifics of its form and possibly even the genre in which it was written, and potentially the intended audience. How in the world can one know all of that without having had the time, for example, to sit down and read the book from cover to cover or to watch the entire movie?

Unfortunately, catalogers do not have the luxury of interacting at length with every item that crosses their desks (a sad fact that has disappointed a number of Cataloging students over the years!). Instead, the technical reading that was described in Chapter 5 as well as some additional attention to the ways the item describes itself will just have to suffice. Simply from the preliminary technical reading, it will be possible to ascertain basics about the topic of a book, its form, and its intended audience, and since it was necessary to do that for the descriptive cataloging anyway, once the descriptive cataloging task is over, it is time to turn to subject cataloging and the subject analysis process.

Subject Analysis

Subject analysis is a process through which the *aboutness* (what the book is about or its topic), the genre and form, and also the audience are assessed. There is a tradition in library and information science where the cataloger is seen as an *information intermediary*. Subject analysis is perhaps the part of professional cataloging where this role as intermediary plays out the most. To carry out subject analysis, the cataloger will attempt to identify information regarding the *aboutness* of the item. Aspects of subject analysis that can help determining the *aboutness* of an item will come from places like the table of contents, the preface, the index, and potentially even the bibliography (what terms appear in the titles of works that are cited?). Some items contain biographical information about the author, and this too can be helpful in ascertaining elements of *aboutness*. In academic libraries and others that track fund codes for purchasing, it may be helpful for the cataloger to know that the item about Wikipedia was requested by a faculty member in the social sciences, and not in the computer science department, since this might provide insight on the approach used by the author.

Information gleaned through the subject analysis process will, in turn, serve as the groundwork for the creation of subject headings and the call number. In essence, the cataloger is working backward from how a future patron will search for the item. The rule of thumb is to bring forth elements of the *aboutness* that are represented in at least 20% of the item. This means that in a book with five chapters, if a single chapter is devoted to ice cream, then ice cream should be included in the subject analysis process (and very likely, a subject heading will be created to convey this idea).

Catalogers look specifically for the following kinds of information:

- the topic of the item (cloud computing, plant biology, a person's life [i.e., a biography/autobiography], kittens, etc.)
- temporal elements relating to the topic of the item (20th century, the U.S. Civil War, the reign of Louis XV in France, etc.)
- geographic location relating to the topic of the item (Milwaukee, the Caribbean, Pakistan, etc.)
- the form of the item (encyclopedia, newspaper, etc.)
- the genre of the item (historical fiction, television series, etc.)
- the intended audience for the item (juvenile, fourth grade reading level, adult, etc.)

Some library textbooks mentioned earlier that cover subject analysis suggest that students in cataloging create a sentence based on their subject analysis. These sentences will include elements that need to be brought forth based on the aspects mentioned above, and help new catalogers organize and formalize their thoughts. In the real world, writing out a sentence every time a cataloger has to catalog a book may not be practical, but going through the process mentally, especially at first, can give an idea of the breadth and complexity of elements to be included in the bibliographic record.

BIAS AND SUBJECT ANALYSIS

In cataloging, it is important to record faithfully and without bias information about the items being cataloged. Unbiased representation is somewhat straightforward in descriptive cataloging where the cataloger is transcribing the words that appear on the title page (or somewhere else on the item) or recording information that is evident from looking at the item critically and with a trained eye.

Subject analysis is different because it requires the cataloger to interpret the information in the resource. With nonfiction for children, this might be straightforward: the item is about guppies. Period. With materials for adults, however, even nonfiction can be a challenge if the author's intent involves persuasion or deception, if it is unclear the level for which the material was conceived, or even how novel concepts like cutting edge research fit into the classification schemes we currently have in place.

With subject analysis as with other parts of cataloging, there is no point in agonizing. Best practices and tradition instruct catalogers to be aware of their biases (and, as professionals, to be neutral when assessing topicality and providing access based on *aboutness*), to make the best guess possible, to see what the Library of Congress (LC) has done in similar cases if necessary, and to move on.

Controlled Vocabulary Access Points for Subject Access

Librarians have created controlled vocabularies for subject terms the same way they have for name access points such as Shakespeare, William, 1564–1616. Within the structure of the *Functional Requirements for Bibliographic Records* (FRBR) user tasks of find, identify, select, and obtain, controlled vocabularies providing terms related to subject access have the potential to help users find, identify, and even select items based on their information needs.[1] Classification numbers and call numbers assist with obtaining, and potentially with finding, identifying, and selecting as well.

Controlled Vocabularies

Controlled vocabularies are sophisticated lists of terms that catalogers consult when creating access points in bibliographic records. The lists of name authorities we saw in Chapter 7 are, themselves, kinds of controlled vocabularies. When subject cataloging, catalogers will use the term as it appears in the controlled vocabulary (i.e., *Jewelry making*) to represent a concept in the bibliographic record. Users can then find the record for the item, along with records for any other item on that same topic, by searching the controlled vocabulary term in the online catalog.

Controlled vocabularies also list synonyms that should not be used, even though the synonyms are legitimate terms. The point of the controlled vocabulary is to identify which one of the synonyms will be used! At times, scope notes, or instructions to the cataloger, are included to help with the systematic use of the vocabulary by all catalogers everywhere.

One type of controlled vocabulary is the *thesaurus*. Thesauri not only list words that should be used (i.e., authorized terms) by the cataloger but also provide additional information about the terms and their hierarchical relationship to other terms in the thesaurus. Three main types of relationships can be identified: broader terms, narrower terms, and related terms. Broader terms (BT) are hierarchically "parents" to the term. For example, Vans is a BT to Minivans since minivans are a type of van. Narrower terms (NT) are hierarchically a "child" to the term, meaning that they are more specific term. An example is *Manicure scissors,* an NT to *Scissors and shears* in LCSH. Related terms (RT) will have a *See also* relationship. *Bodybuilding* and *Weight training* are both nuanced terms and are authorized access points in their own right, but there is a close relationship of meaning between the two. Accordingly, in LCSH, they have a RT relationship.

LCSH IN THEORY: PRINCIPLES BEHIND THE HEADINGS

LCSH is probably the most common controlled vocabulary used in libraries in the United States. LCSH is technically a subject heading list, not a thesaurus, maintained by the Library of Congress (LC). The terms in LCSH are devised by experts at LC and are based on *literary warrant.* Since librarians need to find a neutral way to devise terms, they have decided to create the LCSH terms based on the words in the items held in the library. The *warrant* is literary because it is based on the published *literature,* primarily in LC's collection. For this reason, areas where LC collects heavily tend to be well represented in LCSH.

When there is a colloquial term and a learned term, however, authors publishing in books that are collected by LC will tend to use the learned term. This means that LCSH terms can sound stodgy, and even outdated, especially if the terms in the controlled vocabulary are not revisited and updated for long periods of time.

LCSH terms tend to be given in the plural if they designate things that can be counted (e.g., Cats, Horses); ideas tend to be given in the singular (e.g., Philosophy). For this reason, we know that the LCSH term *Theater* is about the concept of putting on plays, not about the buildings that house the plays (i.e., Theaters).

Catalogers use LCSH terms as they are—no doctoring allowed. If a term is arcane or even mildly offensive, catalogers will still use it anyway. Catalogers are not insensitive to their patrons, but must adhere to the standards as part of their professional work. Terms can and do change over time, primarily when the literary warrant permits.

The principle of *specific entry* dictates that the cataloger supply only the most specific term for a topic in the catalog record. If a cataloger has a book about growing heirloom tomatoes, then only the most specific subject heading should be used. Additional headings about gardening in general or plant biology are too broad and should not be supplied in addition to the specific term.

In LCSH, catalogers are not allowed to invent terms, even if it makes sense (i.e., even if they have a book in front of them on the topic). If a specific term does not exist, catalogers will need to find a way to use a hierarchically broader term or to supply two or more terms that each capture an aspect of the topic until a more specific term can be created by LC.

SACO

The Subject Authority Cooperative Program (SACO) (pronounced *say-co*) is another Program for Cooperative Cataloging (PCC) program that assists with the grassroots creation of headings in LCSH. Normally, LCSH terms are created by experts at LC based on literary warrant, or the appearance of the terms in the materials that LC collects. LC is a depository library, meaning that two copies of every copyrightable book published in the United States are supposed to be sent to LC. Unfortunately, however, not every book made available is represented in the collection, no matter how hard LC tries. Self-published books, theses and dissertations, and other unique and possibly cutting-edge materials may not make it to LC. Additionally, the establishment of subject heading terms can take a while. All of this means that subject headings may not exist when a cataloger goes to assign headings.

Enter the SACO program! SACO permits catalogers to make a case for the creation of new terms based on the materials they are actually cataloging. http://classificationweb.net/Menu/subject.html is where SACO catalogers submit a request and supply documentation supporting the request.

Of course, it is not possible to use a heading until it is formally established by LC, but with SACO, at least, catalogers have a sense of helping things move along based on their own collections.

LCSH Features

LCSH terms all begin with a capital letter. Each subdivision and proper noun will also begin with a capital letter. In catalog records, subject headings end with a period or a terminal mark of punctuation (often, a closing parenthesis).

LCSH terms are unique. When terms could be mistaken for a synonym (e.g., *frames* could be a computer science term, an optometry term, a museum studies term) a qualifier is usually used to provide additional context. These qualifiers generally follow the terms and are included in parentheses. They are part of the heading, and cannot be left off in cataloging.

Sometimes, LCSH terms will be much more complex than a single word. Some terms include two or more words, sometimes with conjunctions like *and,* with words in parentheses, or even words out of order (i.e., inverted) with a comma separating the words, such as *Art, Abstract.* When an institution decides to use LCSH, it is only possible to use the authorized terms from the subject heading list in the bibliographic records. As mentioned, making up terms if they are not available in LCSH is unfortunately not allowed, and altering terms to better suit one's patrons is also not permitted. The only exception is that proper nouns (e.g., names) can be used as subject headings even if there is not an authority record.

LCSH terms are topical subject headings. In the days of card catalog cards, it became obvious that a single topical subject heading (or three) was not enough to adequately identify the topics of materials, especially in larger collections. The practice was developed of adding subdivisions to headings—additional specifications about that primary topic.

Not only is it important to find the topic or topics of an item in order to supply subject heading, it is also necessary to identify additional facets of the work that can be brought forth in subdivisions. Although getting the hang of subdivisions at first is a little tricky, with time, catalogers develop a sense of when to include additional subdivisions as part of the subject heading string.

LCSH in Practice

Nowadays, catalogers add as many LCSH terms as necessary to bring forth the *aboutness* of the materials. Sometimes, it might take more than one term to convey a single idea identified during the subject analysis process. Items may be on many topics as well, necessitating multiple headings. Items can have as few as one heading, or as many as 15. It is most likely that items will have between one and three headings, though. With experience, catalogers begin to learn how many headings should be included in a catalog record. When in doubt, it is always possible to find other books on similar topics in LC's online catalog and to use those same subject headings after confirming they are accurate for the item in hand.

It is important to remember that every time a heading is supplied, patrons searching that topic will expect to find a resource that meets their needs. With subject headings, more is not necessarily better. Stop to ask yourself, "Will my future patron be disappointed to find this item after searching for this subject heading?" If the answer is "Yes" or even "Maybe," it is best not to add it.

Where to Find LCSH Terms

The cataloger creating the catalog record will have to assign the subject headings by adding them to the MARC bibliographic record. The terms are freely available through LC's website and are looked up there first. Before being put online, the subject headings were available as print publications. They were lovingly referred to as the big red books since they were hardbound with distinctive red bindings. Now they are only published electronically.

Given the success that LC had with MARC encoding in the computer age, it may not be a surprise that they also use MARC for encoding subject headings. At present, they are also published as linked data, also through the LC website.

Additional services make the headings available for catalogers. Classification Web (http://classificationweb.net), a paid service through LC, provides an easily searchable interface that catalogers can use to identify headings and subdivisions.

Building Out Subject Heading Strings

Subject heading strings in LCSH can be quite long. They always begin with a subject heading. This might seem silly to mention, but *subdivisions* can never stand alone or begin a subject heading.

Once the main subject heading is determined, the cataloger must decide if there are specific aspects to the topic that need to be brought out through the subdivisions. These aspects can either be further topics, geographical, chronological, or form. If there is more than one subdivision, the order is based on general principles and, in some situations, the idea being conveyed. The one constant is that *form subdivisions* (subdivisions that indicate what an item is, e.g., a map, an encyclopedia, fiction) are always last.

The most important thing to note, however, is that subject headings and subdivisions cannot be strung together willy-nilly. Main headings can only be used as a subdivision if there is a note saying they can. Some subdivisions are considered free-floating, which means that they can be added to just about any main heading.

Other subdivisions can be used only under certain types of headings. For instance, precede with Wounds and injuries can be used only as a subdivision under classes of persons, ethnic groups, and individual regions and organs of the body. The subdivision Accidents can be used only under types of industries and under topics where headings involving the term "accidents" have not been established.

Chronological subdivisions can be used only if they have already been established. This is because they are established to coincide with historical/political events of a particular locale. Because of this, it is rare to find a chronological subdivision that exactly matches your item. Instead, choose one or two chronological subdivisions that best correspond to the time period covered in the item.

Subject headings can be divided geographically only when allowed. Please consult the authority record for the heading to see if it indicates that it is possible to subdivide geographically. If it is not indicated, then subdividing geographically is not possible.

Finally, form subdivisions can be added to almost anything, although there are a few individual exceptions because of redundancies.

Many subject heading strings have been *established,* meaning that they have been pre-grouped together and an authority record has been created; many of them, however, have not. If you are unsure that you constructed a subject heading string correctly, check the online LC authority file (http://authorities.loc.gov/). Any time a subject heading is used in their catalog, it is added to the authority website. Headings without a red authorized heading button should be taken with a grain of salt, but they can often give you an idea if you are on the right track or not.

SEARS LIST OF SUBJECT HEADINGS

The *Sears List of Subject Headings* was developed by Minnie Earl Sears in 1923.[2] Sears uses the same principles and format of LSCH, but on a smaller scale. The list was developed for small- and medium-sized libraries who found LCSH to be too detailed for their collections. For instance, LCSH uses both Cats and Kittens, but Sears groups both of these together under Cats. Sears also tends toward natural language rather than inverted headings. Sears Subject Headings are available in a one-volume print edition and are also available online (subscription fee).[3]

CHILDREN'S SUBJECT HEADINGS (CSH)

The LC's Children's Subject Headings (CSH) is the vocabulary used to describe children's materials.[4] Not unlike Sears, CSH is composed of simplified terms as compared to LCSH. The Children's and Young Adults' Cataloging Program (CYAC) (pronounced *kahy-ak* like the boat) is the program responsible for cataloging of children's fiction at LC and for maintaining CSH. It is the modern continuation of the Annotated Card (AC) Program, which was originally begun in 1965 with the intention of *annotating* card catalog cards for children's fiction by providing summaries and kid-friendly subject headings. In this tradition, CYAC is primarily designed to support access to fiction materials. Items not in scope for the CYAC program include nonfiction, folklore, and poetry.[5] Lest nonfiction be left out, CSH are still included on nonfiction materials at LC—they are simply supplied by subject specialists, not by CYAC catalogers.

MARC CODING FOR SUBJECT HEADINGS

The field tag group for subject headings is 6XX. Fields 600, 610, 611, and 630 follow the same patterns and use the same subfields and first indicators as their counterparts in 1XX and 7XX. Two additional fields for subject headings, 650 and 651, are for topical subject headings. If none of the other tags are appropriate, use a 650. 651s are for geographical names. Both of these fields have a blank first indicator.

Second Indicator

The second indicator specifies which thesaurus was used to formulate the subject heading. We talk about the different thesauri in use later in this chapter. For now, we will mention that Library of Congress Subject Headings (LCSH) are second indicator 0 (zero) and Children's Subject Headings (CSH) are second indicator 1. There is not a specific second indicator for Sears. Instead a 7 is used, which means that the source is specified in the body of the MARC field in a specific subfield, the $2. In fact, any time a second indicator 7 is used, the subject heading field must end in a subfield $2. The source code for Sears is, unsurprisingly, $2 sears.

Subfields

As you may expect, there are some subject heading–specific subfields. All subject headings begin with $a. If a subdivision follows the main subject heading, it will be encoded based on the content it contains. $x precedes topical subdivisions. If none of the other subfields are appropriate, use $x. $y is for chronological subdivisions. These can be a year, range of years, or century. They can also be for a named period within a country's history (e.g., Civil War, 1861–1865). $z is for geographical subdivisions, naming locations such as countries or states. $v is for form subdivisions that explain what the material is.

Subdivisions have no specific order, so we are unable to provide you with any kind of cheat sheet for creating subject heading strings. The order usually depends on exactly what the cataloger is trying to convey. This being said, form subdivisions ($v) are always last among the different subdivisions.

Among the subfields, last but not least is the $2 [source code] if a thesaurus like Sears is being used. We discussed the use of the $2 source code earlier where we described the use of the second indicator 7. The following are some examples of subject heading strings that might appear in a bibliographic record.

600 10 $a Shakespeare, William, $d 1564–1616 $x Criticism and interpretation.
600 10 $a Peck, Richard, $d 1934- $v Interviews.
600 10 $a Steinbeck, John, $d 1902–1968. $t Of mice and men.
610 10 $a Missouri. $b General Assembly. $b House of Representatives.
610 20 $a American Library Association.
610 20 $a St. Louis Cardinals (Baseball team)
610 20 $a Challenger (Spacecraft)
611 20 $a Lewis and Clark Expedition $d (1804–1806)
611 20 $a Olympic Games $n (28th : $d 2004 : $c Athens, Greece)
630 00 $a Breakfast at Tiffany's (Motion picture)
630 00 $a Arabian nights $x History $y 20th century.
630 00 $a Bible. $p Corinthians. $l English. $s Authorized.
650 _ 0 $a Running.
650 _ 0 $a Birds $x Nests.
650 _ 0 $a Basketball players $z United States $v Biography.
650 _ 0 $a Popular music $z United States $y 1961–1970.
650 _ 0 $a Flowers $z Missouri $v Identification.
650 _ 1 $a Pigs $v Fiction.
650 _ 7 $a Cowhands. $2 sears
650 _ 7 $a Native Americans $x Religion $z Delaware. $2 sears
651 _ 0 $a Kansas City (Mo.) $x History.
651 _ 0 $a Moon $x Gravity.
651 _ 0 $a Mississippi River $v Juvenile fiction.
651 _ 0 $a McKinley, Mount (Alaska)

GENRE AND FORM HEADINGS

Earlier in this chapter, the *aboutness* of an item was discussed. However, sometimes an item *is* something. This is known as genre. Subject headings tell what an item is about. Genre headings tell what an item is. *Lord of the Rings* is *about* Hobbits (Fictitious characters), but it *is* Fantasy fiction. For many years, this distinction was not made on cataloging records, and both terms would have been lumped together under subject headings.

In 2007, LC decided to make genre and form terms into separate entities from subject headings. Originally the genre terms were separate records with the subject headings, but in 2011 they were moved to their own controlled vocabulary list, *Library of Congress Genre/Form Terms for Library and Archival Materials* (LCGFT). The first projects to be completed were the creation of headings for moving images, radio programs, cartographic materials, and law materials. These projects were complete by 2010. General, music, and literature terms were released in early 2015. Religion terms are being devised at the time of writing and may be completed by the end of 2015, and the art terms project has recently begun. In MARC, LCGFT are input in 655 _7. "$2 lcgft" is added after the genre/form term. It is important to keep in mind that most genre headings are also valid as subject headings. So if you have a book *about* science fiction, you would code "Science fiction" as a 650, not 655.

A related project is the *Library of Congress Medium of Performance Thesaurus for Music* (LCMPT). These terms describe the instruments and voices used in musical works. Genre and form terms should be added as appropriate to records.

CONCLUSION

Specifying what an item is about and what it is in a systematic way is essential for providing the kind of access to materials that patrons expect and deserve. Subject headings, especially LCSH, are complex, but their careful crafting is worth the effort. With the addition of other vocabularies like the LCGFT, libraries are able to provide even better, more precise access to materials based on not only what they are about, but what they are.

NOTES

1. International Federation of Library Associations, & Institutions. Section on Cataloguing. Standing Committee. (1998). *Functional requirements for bibliographic records: final report* (Vol. 19). IFLA Study Group on the Functional Requirements for Bibliographic Records (Ed.). KG Saur Verlag Gmbh & Company. http://www.ifla.org/files/assets/cataloguing/frbr/frbr_2008.pdf (Accessed March 1, 2015)
2. Sears List of Subject Headings. 2014. H. W. Wilson. 978-1-61925-190-8
3. Sears List of Subject Headings. 2015. http://www.ebscohost.com/academic/sears-list-of-subject-headings
4. Children's Subject Headings (CSH) List. 2015. Children's and Young Adults' Cataloging Program (CYAC), Library of Congress. http://loc.gov/aba/cyac/childsubjhead.html (accessed April 7, 2015)
5. About the Program. 2015. Children's and Young Adults' Cataloging Program (CYAC), Library of Congress. http://loc.gov/aba/cyac/about.html (accessed February 26, 2015)

SUGGESTED RESOURCES

Library of Congress. 2014. H 1095 Free-Floating Subdivisions. In *Subject Headings Manual.* Available at http://www.loc.gov/aba/publications/FreeSHM/H1095.pdf

Library of Congress. n.d. Subject Cataloging Training Guide. 3rd rev. ed. Available through Cataloger's Desktop (http://desktop.loc.gov).

Library of Congress. n.d. Subject Headings Manual. 1st ed. Available at http://www.loc.gov/aba/publications/FreeSHM/freeshm.html

CHAPTER 9

Classification

This chapter describes some of the nitty-gritty of library classification, including the creation of call numbers. We start by talking about classification and thinking about the anatomy of a call number. Then, we look more closely at Dewey Decimal Classification (DDC), known by most as Dewey, and finally at Library of Congress Classification (LCC).

Classification is another method of organizing materials; as with supplying subject headings, classifying is based primarily on the intellectual contents, or what the materials are about. Subject analysis is carried out in the creation of subject heading; it also informs the creation of classification numbers based on the classification scheme in use. Most patrons know call numbers as the numbers affixed to the spines of library books, but patrons may not give thought to the process of creating and supplying them, or even to the different parts that compose them.

Call numbers provide a unique shelf location for library materials. In the past, library stacks (i.e., shelves) were closed and books were organized in the order that they were acquired. Books about the history of Ancient Greece could potentially be shelved between books about childhood diseases and astronomy. There was no meaningful order to the way books were organized, other than when they entered the library, but it did not matter since patrons were unable to browse the shelves and find their own books. John Cotton Dana is credited with the democratization of the public library through his abolition of the closed-stack system in the late 1800s and open access to materials for children.[1] Academic and research libraries were already opening up before this time, with DDC, which allows for browsing, first being published in 1876. Today, most libraries in the United States have open stacks, and the materials are classed by subject, with all books on a given topic, for example, being classed at the same number. Like other aspects of cataloging, call numbers have to be created. Unsurprisingly, they are created according to set standards and professional practice.

Decisions about the classification scheme in use in a library will likely have preceded you—you will work either in a DDC library (mostly public and school libraries) or in a Library of Congress Classification (LCC) library (probably an academic or research library).

CLASSIFICATION AND SHELF LOCATION: CALL NUMBERS

Call numbers are printed on the spines of books or affixed to other materials and represent the principal way materials are organized for retrieval in open-stack environments. Of the two main classification schemes in use in libraries in the United States, DDC and LCC, both work in similar ways. Call numbers will generally follow this simple formula:

classification number + book number + (possible other stuff) = call number

In this section, we break down each of these in turn.

Classification Number

In both DDC and LCC, the cataloger will choose the classification number from what is called the *schedules*. The schedules are lists of possible classification numbers and the topics they represent; often, they are quite detailed. The schedules tend to be organized logically, with similar topics being given similar classification (or *class*) numbers. Thanks to the schedules, catalogers know which topics should be classed where.

The classification portion of the call number, therefore, will be *identical* for every item on a given topic. It makes sense that every book about dogs will be given the same classification number as all of the other books about dogs. This clearly allows for browsing and supports findability and also serendipity.

Since it is likely that a library will have a number of books on dogs, there has to be a way to organize all of the materials with the same class number. Bookstores vaguely put books in order under broad topics based on the author's name. Not every book has an author, however. Some have editors or compilers, and others are written by corporate bodies. Libraries have solved this problem by creating a second number within which books at a class number will be organized. These are called book numbers.

Book Number

The *book number* (or *author number,* or more commonly, the *Cutter number*) is the second part of the call number. It follows the classification number and allows for the books to be organized properly on the shelf. Book numbers were devised by Charles A. Cutter of the *Objects for a Dictionary Catalog* fame.[2]

All Cutter numbers are based on the notion known as the *primary access point* (called *main entry* in former cataloging rules). The primary access point was, in the days of card catalog cards, the main card catalog card associated with a book. Each book would have a number of entries on cards, including entries for authors, the title of the book and possibly for the series, and subject cards. The primary access point was generally associated with the author's name written in the last-name-first fashion in which it appears as an access point.

Book numbers are based either on the first-named author on an authored work or on the title if there is no author. The few minor exceptions to these rules will be discussed later, but for the most part, using the first-named author's last name (as it appears in the MARC 100 field), and if there is not one (e.g., if there is an editor), just using the title as the basis for the book number will be fine 98% of the time.

Cutter's book numbers do two things, and they do them well:

1. "collapse" letters from words/names into numbers for ease of shelf organization
2. facilitate alphabetization, especially important with last names beginning with, for example, Sch, which would be difficult to organize meaningfully based on the relatively small number of characters that fit easily on the spine label

You may be catching on that Cutter numbers, like class numbers, are the work of the cataloger. Whereas in creating class numbers, catalogers consult schedules, in creating book numbers, catalogers need to consult *tables*. The table chosen will be, in part, a function of the classification scheme in use. For DDC, it might also be a question of practice. Entries on Cutter's original list had only one letter and two digits. Since that time, a number of individuals and organizations have revised and expanded the list to better accommodate larger collections. Librarians using DDC can use whichever version they wish, and again, this will likely have been chosen long before your arrival.

Despite some differences, all book numbers begin with the first letter(s) of the primary access point. Then, the remaining letters are condensed using the chosen table and turned into numbers that can fit relatively easily onto a spine label. For example, according to the Cutter Sanborn Four–Figure Table, S5272 is the Cutter number for the playwright William Shakespeare. But, using the Cutter Four-Figure Table, Sh152 is the Cutter number. As long as a library is consistent, the system works beautifully.

After Cutter numbers based on an author, a lowercase work mark is added. This corresponds to first word of the title (skip initial articles). So Hamlet would be S5272h and Macbeth would be S5272m in a Cutter Sanborn Four–Figure library. Cutter numbers based on a title do not receive a work mark. Cutter numbers for biographical works are treated differently and are discussed next.

Some librarians prefer to use either the author's last name or a portion of the author's last name as a book number (e.g., Shakespeare or Shakes). While this is valid, it means that call numbers will probably not be unique, nor will they necessarily fit well on the spine.

Other Content in Call Numbers

Finally, other content can be included in the completed call number beyond just the classification number and the book number. The addition of extra content is dictated by the classification scheme in use. For example, LCC requires dates in all call numbers, but DDC requires them only in certain cases. LCC might also have additional Cutter numbers, not for the primary access point but as part of the classification number itself. In the case of multiple volumes, v. or vol. plus the number will generally be used. Some librarians hold to the long-standing tradition of ensuring that call numbers are completely unique. To do this when they hold multiple copies of the same item, a librarian will add c. 2 to the second copy received, c. 3 to the third copy received, and so on. Other librarians opt to use barcodes to differentiate identical items with identical call numbers.

DDC: PRINCIPLES AND PRACTICE

DDC, also known as *Dewey* to patrons and librarians alike, has in some ways come to be synonymous with library organization. DDC can be used in libraries of any size, with the abridged version, *Abridged Dewey,* more suited to smaller libraries holding fewer than 20,000 volumes.

Full *Dewey,* the standard version of DDC, is available as one very compact four-volume set or as an online product through OCLC. *Abridged Dewey* is available the same way, but is only a single volume in its print form.

DDC is designed to organize the whole of human knowledge. When you think about it, this is a really big task! Everything in DDC is base-ten and hierarchical. Each of the ten main classes is subdivided into ten subdivisions, each of these into ten more subdivisions. Subclasses retain all of the characteristics of the broader hierarchical class; they are simply more specific.

Practically speaking, this means that the longer the number in DDC, the more specific it is. All DDC numbers have at least three places, with zeros as placeholders if need be. In this way, materials classed at 330 are more specific than materials classed at 300.

DDC makes extensive use of mnemonics and repetition with the numbers. Numbers representing geographic locations, for example, are repeated whenever that location is brought forth in a number. Books about French literature, travel in France, French cooking, and French politics all have the potential to contain the series of numbers that represent France (-44). One drawback of DDC is that the more specific a number is, the longer it probably will be. In the cases of the examples with France earlier, smaller libraries may not feel the need to create long and precise classification numbers called *close classification* if their collections are not extensive in that area. These libraries may be content with broad classification, less precise, shorter numbers, to designate the place of their books.

Finally, DDC organizes by discipline, with facets such as form of the materials and geographic location being added, potentially, to the base number. See Sidebar 9.1 for more information about disciplines in DDC.

SIDEBAR 9.1   PRO TIP: ORGANIZING BY DISCIPLINE IN DEWEY

What does it really mean to organize by discipline? Remember, Melvil Dewey got his start in an academic library, and academic institutions do this all the time. Students doing work in vision may find their home in a number of academic disciplines. Some may be in the arts (701.8), others in epistemology (121.35); some might be in artificial intelligence (006.37), with yet others in human physiology (612.84) or psychology (152.14). Vision may be the topic, but the approach will be different based on the discipline.

DDC works much the same way. A book about vision will be classed with the discipline in which it is studied. More information about this is available in the introduction to Dewey (p. xli–xlv).

Features of DDC

DDC is a *decimal* classification; this means it is as if the entire class number were following an invisible decimal. Even though there is a decimal before the fourth digit (if indeed there is a fourth digit), the *entire* DDC number is a decimal!

Grade school math teaches that the number immediately following the decimal is in the tens place, the second column over is the hundreds, and the third column beyond the decimal is the thousands. This, believe it or not, is the terminology that DDC uses as well.

DDC's decimals and standard numbers involving decimals have two main differences than decimals in grade school mathematics:

- DDC numbers are not preceded by a decimal, but after the thousands column, a decimal is added for readability (e.g., 743.69752).
- DDC numbers will always have a minimum of three digits, meaning sometimes DDC numbers add a zero to the hundreds and/or thousands place (e.g., 500 for a book about science in general).

Like standard numbers involving decimals in mathematics, DDC numbers will never end with a zero after the decimal.

Mechanics of DDC

DDC is published every seven years in print and is updated regularly in the online product, WebDewey. The print version of standard DDS is, as stated earlier, composed of four volumes. In the 23rd edition, published in 2011, the volumes are organized in the following way:

> volume 1: introduction, glossary, manual, tables
> volume 2: schedules from 000 to 599
> volume 3: schedules from 600 to 999
> volume 4: relative index

In volume 1, the introduction is very helpful in situating the work that is done in classification and in understanding how to implement DDC. Since DDC does use a bit of its own vocabulary, the glossary will also be very helpful to those striking out with DDC on their own for the first time. The manual, also in volume 1, helps clarify which classification number to use if there are two or more logical choices. Finally, the tables allow catalogers to construct longer and more specific classification numbers than what is already built out in the schedules. This is a major feature of DDC!

Volumes 2 and 3 are the schedules themselves. Schedules are the numerical listing of classification numbers along with the topics they represent and basic instructions for applying them.

DDC is an amazing exercise in organizing knowledge, with immediate applications for organizing library materials. DDC numbers are hierarchical: the shorter the number, the broader the topic. Items classed at 500 are about science in general; items at 570 are about biology; and items at 572 are about biochemistry. All of the traits inherent in the grandparent 500 are evident in the more specific child 570 and in the yet more specific grandchild 572. This allows for a great deal of compactness when presenting the schedules.

Because of its compactness, with DDC, it is necessary for the cataloger to look back to previous numbers in the hierarchy in order to understand if the number they have selected is in the correct broad discipline. The tables, additionally, allow for catalogers to *build* classification numbers beyond what is available in the schedules.

Tables in DDC

To build numbers in DDC, one uses tables. There are six tables in full DDC and four tables in abridged DDC. Tables 1–4 are the same in both versions.

Table 1 is for *standard subdivisions* in DDC lingo. These act somewhat like the free-floating subdivisions for subject headings. Standard subdivisions are common aspects or forms that are found in all disciplines. For the most part, they can be added to almost any number, although there are some exceptions. Examples of standard subdivisions are philosophy and theory (—01), dictionaries/encyclopedias (—03), and study and teaching (—07). The dashes in front of the numbers mean that they need to be added to another number. Note that the dashes do not appear in the built number. If this is an encyclopedia of croquet, add—03 to the number for croquet (796.354), with the final class number being 796.35403.

Table 2 is for geographic areas, historical periods, and biography, but is mostly used for the geographic aspects. Every country in the world has its own number. A number of countries have further subdivisions for states, provinces, and so on. Full DDC lists further subdivisions down to the county/district level for select countries and provides numbers for very large cities. These numbers are used as the basis for most of the numbers in the 900s. They can also be added to the end of other numbers, either directly (where the instructions allow) or after the -09 subdivision from table 1.

Table 3 is used only with the 800s and only when allowed. Table 3 brings out aspects of individual literatures and specific literary forms. Many of the numbers that use table 3 have already been built in the schedules.

Table 4 is used only with numbers from 420 to 499 and only when allowed. As with table 3, many of the numbers that use table 4 are already in the schedules.

Table 5 only appears in full *Dewey*. It lists ethnic and national groups. These numbers can only be used directly when the instructions in the schedules allow or after the -089 subdivision from table 1.

Table 6 is also unique to full *Dewey*. It is for languages and is only used when the instructions specifically say to use table 6.

Author Numbers in DDC: Principles and Practice

Book numbers in DDC are based on the primary access point. Generally, book numbers are created based on either one of the Cutter tables or one of the Cutter-Sanborn tables. OCLC has created a freely downloadable Cutter program that works on PCs. When using it, it important to input both the last name and the first name. For example, Smith is a common last name. The table will produce a different book number for Jane Smith than for Sam Smith. See Figure 9.1 for a screenshot of the OCLC Dewey Cutter Program in action.

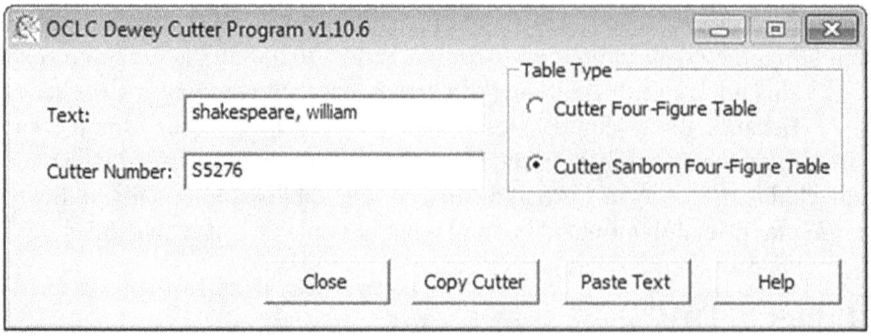

Figure 9.1 OCLC Dewey Cutter Program.

DDC: Special Cases

Fiction and biography pose some unique problems in DDC. There are a few different ways these items can be cataloged, but most librarians tend to follow practices that are already in place unless there is a compelling reason to change. Generally, documentation will be available to guide the cataloger's work, but sometimes there is not a good written explanation. The following are a few scenarios that may give additional insight into the practice at your institution for these kinds of materials.

According to the schedules, items that are works of fiction (other than folklore) belong in the 800s. Fiction is further classed by the country of origin of the author, with American novels, for example, classed in the 813, and British novels in 823. More complex numbers can be built out that include aspects relating to the timeframe during which the book was written or aspects relating to the genre or general topics (e.g., vampire fiction). The Cutter number will be for the author of the novel, and in the case of voluminous authors or authors whose works have been edited and studied, a date may be used to differentiate editions.

Some librarians will choose to place all novels in a Fiction class, sometimes designated by the letter F or by Fic. in lieu of a class number. Items in fiction sections will be organized by the author's last name. These librarians might also opt not to use book numbers, but instead to alphabetize more or less based on the first three letters of the author's last name. This is certainly not the recommended method since it does not adhere to the standards, yet you may find that you inherit such a system and need to continue the practice.

It might be tempting to "fix" the items so that they are organized better. When thinking in terms of the entire collection, however, this would take a very long time. Even if one person could dedicate all of his or her time to it, which is unlikely, the project has the potential to be overwhelming. To change the call number, the books would have to be pulled off the shelves, the new numbers figured out, the call number would need to be changed in the cataloging record, the spine labels created, printed, and affixed, and finally the books would need to be re-shelved. Another option would be to not change what is already in the collection, but use a new system going forward on the new items, hoping that weeding will eventually get rid of all the old numbers. However, you will need to decide if two numbering systems would be confusing to your patrons and if your own sanity can withstand dealing with the two systems.

Books about people also get special consideration in DDC. There are two primary choices for classing biography: either biography is classed in the 920s (with history) or it is assigned a B (for *Biography*). In both cases, the Cutter number is for the subject of the biography, and the work mark is for the author.

Encoding DDC in MARC

DDC numbers are encoded in MARC in the 082 Dewey Decimal Classification Number. This field is repeatable, so there can be more than one DDC number in a record you might find while doing copy cataloging. In this case, you will need to decide which number to use in your library. The following are examples of full DDC class numbers (first indicator 0) created at LC (second indicator 0) or elsewhere (second indicator 4) encoded in MARC.

When there is a slash (i.e., 650.1/1), the cataloger will need to decide whether to use the broad classification (i.e., 650.1) or whether the library's collection is large enough to warrant the closer classification at 650.11. Dewey is currently in the 23rd edition, so when catalogers see numbers from earlier editions (i.e., $2 22 or earlier edition), the cataloger will want to confirm that the class number is still valid.

082 00 $a 650.1/1 $2 22
082 00 $a 791.43/095 $2 23
082 04 $a 597.89 $2 23
082 04 $a 976.4/002 $2 22
082 00 $a 332.6 $2 23
082 00 $a 641.6/71476 $2 23

Generally, even though libraries share records and DDC classification numbers, they tend not to share their Cutter numbers. When importing copy, if you work in a Dewey library, you will need to add the Cutter number yourself according to the table your library uses.

LCC: PRINCIPLES AND PRACTICE

LCC is the other main classification scheme used in the United States. LCC, as its name implies, is maintained by LC. Since LC is a research collection *par excellence,* LCC is usually used to organize the books of academic and research libraries. LCC does not intend to classify the whole of human knowledge—it simply aims to organize the books on the shelves of a large research library. Literary warrant, therefore, influences the creation of class numbers, and the rigid adherence to hierarchy and a base-ten system of DDC does not play a part in LCC.

Features and Mechanics of LCC

Like DDC, LCC is also applied by the cataloger and the numbers are taken from schedules with the intention of grouping like items on the shelves. Although its function as a classification scheme is similar to that of Dewey's, the features and mechanics of LCC are somewhat different.

Instead of being analytico-synthetic like Dewey, where catalogers build numbers extensively, LCC is largely enumerative, meaning that catalogers simply select the class number that applies from the schedules; no building necessary for the most part.

Another difference is that, instead of having 10 main classes like DDC, LCC has 21 main classes. Many of these classes have subdivisions. Given that LC needs to organize materials that inform military operations, entire classes are devoted to the Military Science (U) and to Naval Science (V).

Whereas DDC classification numbers are made up exclusively of Arabic numerals, LCC class numbers have both letters and numbers. Additionally, the numbers in LCC are whole numbers, unless they follow a period. Who cares about the difference between whole numbers and decimals? Although on the surface it seems like a minor difference that might only be useful on trivia night, it affects shelving and ultimately retrieval. This is because HF59.7 .B55 1987 precedes HF5823 .K38 2013 (i.e., the number 59.7 comes before the number 5823) in LCC. In DDC, however, 629.13 files before 629.3 (i.e., .1 comes before .3).

Author Numbers in LCC: Principles and Practice

LCC schedules are different from DDC schedules, so it may not be surprising that LCC book numbers are still Cutter numbers, but they are created with a different Cutter table. The Cutter table used in LCC fits on a single page and is used to devise a unique shelf address, again based on the primary access point. The first letter of the author's last name will guide the choice of the first number, and subsequent letters will guide the rest. Most LCC libraries build out one letter and two or three numbers, the goal always being to situate the book on the shelf, within the class number, while maintaining the alphabetical order of the last names of authors.

Library holdings are different from library to library. When doing copy cataloging, catalogers always start with the Cutter number in the record (normally, there will be one). The thing is the Cutter number in cataloging copy is devised to organize that item in the LC's collection or in some other collection. Local collections may have items not held in the LC, so local adjustments to the Cutter number will need to be made.

Before assigning the LCC call number, the item needs to be *shelflisted*. In shelf listing, the cataloger will make sure that the Cutter number for the item being catalogued correctly (i.e., alphabetically) places the item on the shelf, amongst all of the other items with the same class number. Sometimes, this means the cataloger will need to adjust the Cutter number. See Figure 9.2 for the LC Cutter table used with LCC.

Cutter table

Below is a short Cutter table (taken from *Subject Cataloging Manual : Shelflisting* instruction sheet G 60) for use as a guide.

Note: the final Cutter number is based on entries already found in the shelflist (and in some cases entries reserved for other libraries for which LC does not have an item in its catalog).

The letters in the table represent the letter that follows the initial letter of the author's surname (vowel, consonant, etc.). The number is that which should be used; however, it may be necessary to add other numbers or to use judgement to allow for growth when providing numbers for extremely common names.

Generally Cutter numbers do not end with the numeral 1or 0.

1. After initial vowel								
for the second letter:	b	d	l-m	n	p	r	s-t	u-y
use number:	2	3	4	5	6	7	8	9

2. After initial letter S								
for the second letter:	a	ch	e	h-i	m-p	t	u	w-z
use number:	2	3	4	5	6	7	8	9

3. After initial letters Qu							
for the second letter:	a	e	i	o	r	t	y
use number:	3	4	5	6	7	8	9

For initial letters Qa-Qt, use 2-29

4. After other initial consonants							
for the second letter:	a	e	i	o	r	u	y
use number:	3	4	5	6	7	8	9

5. For expansion						
for the second letter:	a-d	e-h	i-l	m-o	p-s	t-v	w-z
use number:	3	4	5	6	7	8	9

Figure 9.2 LC Cutter Table.[3]

For example, if Cuttering for Sandy, the cataloger will use the S, and add to it the digit 2 (representing the "a"), followed by the digit 6 to represent the n, and possibly a 3 to represent the d. The LC Cutter for Sandy, then, is either S26 or S263.

LCC: Special Cases

The special cases mentioned for DDC, fiction and biography, are not really noteworthy in LCC. Fiction is classed in the Ps, also by author's nationality. Because a number of authors come from a given country, generally Cutter numbers for the author's names are included as part of the classification number. In these cases, a second Cutter (used as a book number) is added based on the title.

Biography is classed with the topic, not separately, in LCC, so no additional considerations for biography need to be kept in mind. One aspect of classing in LCC that may be challenging to the non-specialist is the Ks, where legal decisions are classed.

Encoding LCC in MARC

Like the DDC number in a MARC record, the LCC field, the MARC 050, is repeatable. And, there is nothing that precludes there from being both an LCC number and a DDC number in the same record—in fact, it is quite common. The following numbers were all LCC numbers created at LC (second indicator 0). The Cutter number for the author is in the $b followed by the date of publication (or copyright). Only the first Cutter number is preceded by a period. If there is a Cutter number as part of the classification number (as in TX759.5.Y63), the second Cutter number, the book number, will not be preceded by a period.

```
050 00 $a HG179 $b .P44728 2015
050 00 $a TX759.5.Y63 $b A45 2014
050 00 $a QL644.2 $b .A43 2015
050 00 $a TT395 $b .V66 2013
050 00 $a PR502 $b .F36 2006
```

ANOTHER CLASSIFICATION SCHEME: SUDOCS

Government documents collections may not be classed using DDC or LCC, even if the rest of the items in the library are. Government documents collections tend to use the Superintendent of Documents Classification Scheme (SuDocs). SuDocs numbers are not created by the cataloging librarian, as they are not based on the topicality of the work. Instead, SuDocs numbers are generated, generally by government documents librarians, and designed to group documents based on the organization that issued them.[4]

OTHER METHODS OF ORGANIZING: ACCESSION NUMBERS

For materials that are not located in open-stack environments, the decision may be made not to provide a topic-based class number. As an example, audiovisual materials may be given an accession number. Patrons wishing to request the material will supply the accession number to librarians after having found it in the catalog. Other options might include some variant, with materials of a certain format being placed wholesale at a particular class number or call number and then differentiated by some additional number, Cutter number, date, and so on.

CONCLUSION

It is not enough to describe materials and to provide verbal subject in the catalog—items must be classified so that they can be retrieved. By virtue of the classification scheme's structure, items on similar topics are placed in proximity to each other on the shelves. When books on similar topics are close to each other physically, this promotes the serendipitous discovery of materials patrons did not know were there, and may never have found otherwise!

Given the complexity of information retrieval issues today, cutting corners on classification is not a good idea. Additionally, when schemes are used and applied consistently, records can be shared. As catalogers are wont to say, the future is longer than the past. It is impossible to know which systems will be in use in a given library in the future, what kind of effort will be needed to crosswalk today's data and make it usable in tomorrow's systems. By adhering to standards, including for classification, librarians have a much better chance of seeing their data successfully move forward into the future.

NOTES

1 Kevin Mattson. 2000. "The Librarian as Secular Minister to Democracy: The Life and Ideas of John Cotton Dana." *Libraries & Culture*, 35(4): 514–534.
2. For more information, see the introduction to G 63 Cutter Numbers in the *Classification and Shelflisting Manual*, available at http://www.loc.gov/aba/publications/FreeCSM/G063.pdf
3. The version shown here is from LC NACO's website: http://loc.gov/aba/pcc/053/table.html The LC Cutter Table can also be found in *Classification and Shelflisting Manual*, instruction sheet G63, 2008 ed.
4. To learn more about the SuDocs scheme, visit the Federal Depository Library Program (FDLP) website: http://www.fdlp.gov/catalogingandclassification/cataloging-articles/1791-superintendent-of-documents-sudocs-classification-scheme

SUGGESTED RESOURCES

Classification Web (subscription service for accessing Library of Congress Classification schedules). n.d. Library of Congress. https://classificationweb.net/

Library of Congress. 2013. Classification and Shelflisting Manual. 2013 ed. Available at http://www.loc.gov/aba/publications/FreeCSM/freecsm.html

Library of Congress. 2008. G 63 Cutter Numbers. In *Classification and Shelflisting Manual*. Available at http://www.loc.gov/aba/publications/FreeCSM/G063.pdf

Melvil Dewey. 2011. "Dewey Decimal Classification and Relative Index" (JS Mitchell, J. Beall, R. Green, G. Martin, & M. Panzer, Eds.). Dublin, OH: OCLC.

CHAPTER 10

Working with Catalog Records and Materials

Cataloging is not just the application of rules and standards to create high-quality records for library items—it is also the sensible creation or acquisition of these records and the preparation of materials for use by patrons. In this chapter, we describe some typical procedures and processes in cataloging departments. We begin by describing procedures for acquiring records that have already been created, and then move to discussing how catalog departments ensure that materials are ready to be shelved and made available.

COPY CATALOGING AND SOURCES OF RECORDS

Most of the cataloging that libraries do is copy cataloging. Catalogers elsewhere create the records, and catalogers locally modify them to make them adhere to local practice in describing local collections. But how does one get these records in the first place? There are three main sources for acquiring bibliographic records used in copy cataloging: cataloging utilities, Z39.50 services, and vendors. The following section will describe each of these in turn, and will conclude with a discussion of the cataloging in publication program that supports the creation of records.

Cataloging Utilities

A cataloging utility is simply a collective depository of cataloging records that then can be downloaded by member libraries. In the United States, there are currently two such utilities, the Online Computer Library Center, Inc. (OCLC) and SkyRiver. OCLC has been around, in some form, since the 1970s. SkyRiver is a newcomer and has only been around since 2009.[1] Both cataloging utilities work in the same basic way. First, an item is searched in the database in an attempt to find a record for it. This may be easier said than done, since there can be similar records for what appears to be a single item (see Sidebar 10.1).

SIDEBAR 10.1   CHOOSING AMONG BIBLIOGRAPHIC RECORDS FOR AN ITEM

When searching for a record to match your item, you may find a number of records that seem to be identical matches. This can be frustrating and confusing—which one should you choose? Luckily, there are a few rules of thumb for choosing a good record. When in doubt, it is best to choose a record created by the Library of Congress (MARC field 040 includes the code for the Library of Congress: DLC), a PCC-member library (the MARC 042 will indicate PCC), or a full-level cataloging record (ELvl I in the fixed fields in OCLC). When choosing your record, if possible, you will want to identify a record that was created in a cataloging agency where English is used. This is important because mentions of the pages, the notes, and so on should be in English if at all possible. Another thing to watch for is which format a record describes. Many print books also have an ebook and audiobook form. Each format requires its own record, so you need to make sure you pick the record for the format you have. If none of the records seem to match the item you have, you may need to do original cataloging. OCLC, in efforts to enforce quality control, publishes online information for "When to Input a New Record" (http://www.oclc.org/bibformats/en/input.html). This will help you understand if the record you are tempted to create would be redundant—and whether you should plan to use one of the existing records instead.

There are many ways to search in these databases, and the type of search used will depend on what the item is. An International Standard Book Number (ISBN) can be the most effective search in many cases; if a record cannot be retrieved based on an ISBN search, the title or author or some combination of the two should be used. A hit list will be returned based on the query, and the cataloger will pick the record that best matches the item in hand for eventual inclusion in the local catalog.

The record chosen will need to be edited and saved to the local system before it can be of any use to patrons. The record can either be edited and then downloaded to the integrated library system (ILS) or downloaded and then edited in the ILS, based on the way the system is set up. None of the edits done to the local copy of the record are reflected in the master (original) copy in the cataloging utility. However, it is possible to update and replace a master record under certain conditions, if, for example, the cataloger finds a mistake or if the record is missing important information. The records found in a cataloging utility should be checked carefully. Although a number of records are high quality, there are many that are not, especially for non-book items.

Cataloging utilities are not free, however. Libraries pay a yearly flat fee to search for records in a cataloging utility, based on usage of the utility and number of holdings, or number of records that they upload into their own systems because they *hold* the item. Libraries can receive credits for uploading original cataloging records and for updating or enhancing records.

Z39.50 Cataloging

Z39.50 is a protocol that allows for the sharing of cataloging records primarily by importing MARC records into an ILS. The letter-and-number combination Z39.50 may seem arbitrary, but all of the protocols and standards supported by the National Information Standards Organization of the United States (NISO) relating to libraries begin with Z39.

To use Z39.50, you will need either special software or have an ILS with Z39.50 capabilities. Z39.50 acts like a "back door" into a library catalog. In order to download another library's records, that library has to allow Z39.50 access to its catalog. If it does, though, there is no fee to pay the library providing the record.

As with anything, there are advantages and disadvantages with Z39.50. The primary advantage to using Z39.50 is the cost. Some ILS software does the searching for you (i.e., the search is done from your ILS, not in the target ILS) and may charge a fee for enabling this service. The major disadvantage to using Z39.50 is that you might have to search each library individually, although there are some ILSs that will let you search a handful or so at a time. This means that you have to know which library has the potential to have a record for an item you have. Another disadvantage is that the searching interfaces are very basic, so records for items without an ISBN or items that have numerous editions can be tricky to find.

Fortunately, LC offers Z39.50 access to its collection, so it is possible to download records from them. However, if you are working at a special library, you may have a hard time finding what you need.[2]

Vendors

Records may also be purchased from *vendors,* an umbrella term for a few different scenarios, namely, publishers and jobbers. When publishers act as catalog record vendors they sell records for only the items they publish. A jobber is a wholesaler who brings in items from multiple publishers. In some cases, the jobbers will supply the cataloging record. They also often attach their own control number to records in bibliographic utilities so that you can use that number to find the appropriate record.

For both publishers and jobbers, when an order is filled and materials are sent to a library, a file of corresponding records is sent electronically. Most vendors who offer this service are ones who almost exclusively supply libraries, for example, Follett or Ingram. This service is also usually provided by ebook providers, especially those who sell their ebooks as collections rather than individually.

Another vendor is a third-party vendor. In this case, the vendor only supplies records. When items are ordered from the publisher or the jobber, they are sent to the vendor, who then catalogs them. After they have been cataloged, the items are forwarded to the library. For this type of service, libraries will fill out a profile that gives instructions on how they want items to be cataloged. Usually when this type of service is used, the majority of the items will be cataloged by the vendor.

The last type of vendor cataloging is specialty cataloging. For this type of service, libraries only have a vendor catalog items they are not able to catalog themselves. Most of the time, this involves items in foreign languages, but it can also include non-book items.

Many vendors who offer cataloging also offer a service known as "shelf-ready." If a library uses this service, the vendor will barcode, stamp, apply spine labels and covers, and do other requested processing so that when the item arrives at the library, it is ready to go directly to the shelf. This does not mean, however, that items and their records should not be checked first. Errors do happen. Further information on this follows.

Cataloging-In-Publication (CIP)

Cataloging-In-Publication (CIP) is cataloging information printed in books. It is usually found on the verso (back) of the title page, but may also be found in the back of a book (colophon). The CIP program began in 1971 at LC. The purpose was to provide a preliminary cataloging record so that the book could be cataloged as soon as it arrived in a library, rather than sitting around for weeks waiting for the card sets to arrive. CIP is created for books most likely to be purchased by U.S. libraries, although there are certain scope limitations to the program. Publishers must apply to be a part of CIP and not all qualify. The program's website, http://www.loc.gov/publish/cip/, describes the program in great detail; the section you are reading in this book is a brief summary of the parts you need to know most.

When the program first began, publishers mailed galley proofs to LC. However, now a pre-publication version is submitted by them electronically. Once the cataloging is finished, a copy of the CIP is emailed to the publisher so that it can be printed in the book. Simultaneously, a MARC CIP record is created; this is essentially a very preliminary MARC record for the book. Once the book is published, a complimentary copy is supposed to be sent to LC, who will then upgrade the record, adding any missing information and changing any incorrect information.

Because CIP information is provided before an item is published, it is not a full catalog record. The physical description information (MARC 300 field) is not provided because this information is generally not known at the time CIP is applied for. Other information (as explained next) may also be missing.

While CIP data is useful, it must be checked carefully when being used. Publishers often change the title, the order of the authors, or just about anything else after the CIP has been created. Also, if publishers did not send the full text, but just some of it, the cataloger may not have understood the scope or slant of the book, so the summary, subject headings, or classification may be inaccurate. The cataloger may have also not been aware of bibliographical references, indexes, or accompanying materials.

Since the inception of the program, the CIP has been formatted to look like a card from a card catalog. At least, that is what it is supposed to look like, but not all publishers print it this way. However, in 2014, LC conducted a survey about CIP use and changes librarians would like to see, with changes set to be implemented in summer 2015. LC is also looking into the possibility of adding a QR code to the CIP that will take the user to the record in the LC Catalog. Following are examples of the old format and the new format created by the CIP Advisory Group. LC will be offering training on interpreting and using the new format. Please note that the new format example is current as of the time of writing, but may be changed in the future.

Old format

Juska, Jane.
  Mrs. Bennet has her say / Jane Juska.— Berkley trade paperback edition.
    pages ; cm
  ISBN 978-0-425-27843-7 (softcover)
  1. Young women—England--Fiction. 2. England—Social life and customs—18th
century—Fiction. I. Austen, Jane, 1775–1817. Pride and prejudice. II. Title.
  PS3610.U875M77 2015
  813'.6--dc23   2014048297

New format

Names: Juska, Jane. | Austen, Jane, 1775-1817. Pride and prejudice.
Title: Mrs. Bennet has her say / Jane Juska.
Description: Berkley trade paperback edition. | New York : Berkley Books, 2015.
Identifiers: LCCN 2014048297 | ISBN 978-0-425-27843-7 (softcover)
Subjects: LCSH: Young women—England—Fiction. | England—Social life and customs—
    18th century—Fiction. | BISAC: FICTION / Historical. | FICTION / Romance /
    General. | GSAFD: Regency fiction. | Humorous fiction. | Satire.
Classification: LCC PS3610.U875 M77 2015 | DDC 813/.6—dc23
LC record available at http://www.loc.gov/lccn/2014048297

YOUR UNIQUE INSTITUTION

Every library is different, and every library's users are different. We have made a case throughout this book for adhering to standards. At times, however, it is not clear how best to do that. Also, at times it makes sense to follow established practice at your institution. If things have been done a certain way for years, you inherit a system that is already in place.

Cataloger's Judgment

As catalogers go through the process of creating records inevitably, the standards will not be sufficient for explaining every scenario. We have presented in this book how to apply the standards in cases where things are more or less cut-and-dried. Yet, life (and publishing) can be messy.

The first rule of thumb when presented with a case that seems not to be covered in the standards is to see if someone else has already created best practices to cover this situation. Does your local institution or consortium have a policy in place? Does LC have some documentation that might guide you? Do cataloging records exist in LC for similar circumstances? Even if you are not a member of OCLC, do they provide documentation in *Bibliographic Formats and Standards* that might guide you?

The next step is to make a decision, not to agonize, and to move on. It is literally possible to spend hours, if not weeks, trying to figure out the one and true right way to catalog tricky materials. In the big picture, though, the longer you wait to catalog the piece, the longer patrons are deprived access. It is better to have a record that faithfully describes the resource and that is free of typographical errors and others than to have one that adheres 100% to standards but that took three days to create.

Additionally, many catalogers acknowledge that cataloging is as much art as science. There is often more than one way to address a situation appropriately. Make a go of it, try your best, and move on. Anguishing on your end does nothing in the long run.

Finally, cataloging decisions are reversible in the future. It is a good idea to document what decision you made, and for which resource, so that you can reassess later if you discover a better way to handle it. By documenting what you did, that also permits you to apply the same logic in any future cases.

Local Practice

The notion of documenting practice leads directly into a discussion of local practice. Local practice is the way an institution systematically treats certain situations. This may have to do with the creation of classification numbers (using non-standard Dewey tables, for example), or with putting information about local collections information with subject headings. In fact, local practice can apply to any number of parts of the cataloging process, and it is important to be familiar with local practice when you start cataloging in a place.

Some local practice decisions categorically go against current standards. The rationale is that, as long as a system is internally consistent, there is no trouble. There are two main arguments against this line of thinking, however, beyond the problem with consistency between your catalog and other catalogs that your users will have to learn to navigate.

First, when standards are not followed, it makes sharing records more difficult, both as the sharer and the sharee. You cannot use others' records, and they cannot use yours without certain possibly unexpected adjustments. This seriously undermines the purpose of having standards in the first place!

Second, although it may seem as if your institution is destined to remain on its own forever, the recent past shows that this may not be the case. Increasingly, small libraries are joining forces to offer cataloging services to patrons. Your records may very well be added to the shared records of a local or regional consortium. To promote inter-library loan (ILL) capabilities, you might join a cataloging utility and need to upload your records. Any number of future events might mean that your siloed records of today will become networked records tomorrow.

Catalogers also often say that the future is longer than the past. If you have inherited local practices that might seem questionable going forward, *now* is always a good time to revisit them. If you decide to change the practice, you will likely change from a certain point moving forward. For contents that are easily changed in the cataloging record and that do not involve shelf placement, it might be possible to do a cleanup in the system to update the old local-practice records to the new standards-based practice. For decisions relating to the call number in particular, you will probably just continue to make changes going forward and not change materials already cataloged. At some point the older materials will be weeded, and the new method will be the only one in use.

CATALOGING WORKFLOW

Cataloging workflow, moving items through the process of cataloging them, has many different possibilities. The size of the cataloging department and the source of items and cataloging records will all influence the resulting workflow. The order given here is not meant to be prescriptive, but instead to be a general outline of what needs to be done. Each library will need to figure out what works best for it.

In larger cataloging departments, the placement of items on certain shelves or carts can be used to keep track of what step of the process an item is in. This is not always practical for smaller departments who must keep all of their items on a cart or two. If this is the case, a list of the steps for processing and cataloging of the items should be made and affixed to the cart. As each step is done, it is checked off or initialed. Not only is this helpful if more than one person works with the items, but if you have other duties besides cataloging, it will help you to keep track of where you are in the process when you come back to the cart.

If you are in a library that receives mostly pre-processed items, you will have a very simple workflow. First the record will need to be downloaded into your catalog. This may be done when the record arrives, most likely before the item does, or when the physical item arrives. Then you will need to do a quick check to make sure the item matches the record. This does not need to be full copy cataloging, but the author and title should be checked just to make sure a mix-up did not happen. Then you will need to check that the call number and barcode on the item match the item record. If everything matches, you are ready to send the item to the shelf.

ONLINE MEDIA WORKFLOWS: THE IMPORTANCE OF PROCEDURE

ebooks, e-audiobooks (i.e. downloadable audiobooks) steaming video, and other online media present a special problem when it comes to workflow. When there is a physical item, the cataloger knows that it needs to be cataloged because it shows up in the department. But for online items, there is nothing for the department to receive. In general, a procedure needs to be put in place to notify the cataloger when an online item has been purchased.

In addition to cataloging and acquisitions personnel, systems personnel may need to be notified if a PURL, or proxy URL, needs to be created. As with the workflow of physical items, there are many possibilities, so the *how* is not as important as making sure that the procedure is in place.

If you receive some or all of your items without pre-processing, the workflow is a bit longer and more complicated. Once items are received into the library for cataloging, they are usually organized in some way. Often they are divided by format and then organized by date received. They can also be further subdivided by specific collection. Items are then worked on in a "first in, first out" basis, although certain items may be moved to the front of the queue because of patron requests or popularity of the material.

The in-house cataloging, be it copy cataloging or original cataloging, is generally done by either professional or paraprofessional staff. Generally, copy cataloging is handled by paraprofessional staff, either in Acquisitions or in Cataloging. Original cataloging tends to be done by professional catalogers or experienced paraprofessionals.

The physical processing, that is, applying spine labels, applying barcodes, affixing book covers, stamping, and so on, is usually done by a clerk, student worker, or volunteer. Often, most of the physical processing is done before cataloging, although spine labels are done after. The following are the most common elements of physical processing, although it is up to each library to determine what they want to do.

- Anti-theft materials—
  - electromagnetic strips inserted in the spine of hardcovers and between the pages of paperbacks.
  - circular overlays for CDs and DVDs.
  - radio frequency identification (RFID) are small tags that combine barcodes with security technology. When tags are read by a scanner, they are automatically checked out and desensitized.
  - security cases for multimedia items that fit over the normal cases.
  - Security stripping is usually one of the first steps done in processing. Items can disappear from the cataloging department, so it is important to get them protected as soon as possible. Items like kits, toys, and games are very hard to security strip. Although it is easy to security strip the container, the container could be left on the shelf while the items are removed. The larger items may be individually stripped, but the smaller items cannot be (security strips cannot be cut). Items kept in closed-stacks (librarian retrieves the wanted item for a patron) usually do not get security stripped, but that is up to the individual library.
- Barcodes—Placement of the barcodes are decided by individual libraries, but the most common places are the inside or outside of the back cover/back of container. Protective covers can also be placed over them. The actual barcode is put on the container for discs. Each disc is then given a ring label with the barcode number and, usually, the name of the library.
- Library stamp—Ownership stamps make the identification of library materials very easy. The most common places to stamp books are the top, bottom, and non-spine side of the book, title page, and inside the back cover. Often libraries will have multiple-sized stamps for varying thickness of books. Discs are not stamped directly, but ring labels are put in the center. These can be either stamped or pre-printed and often include the barcode number. Other items may be labeled or have the ownership written by hand. Other stamps can indicate if an item is non-circulating, damaged, discarded, or withdrawn.
- Covers—Covering books can be expensive, but doing so can help extend the life of a book.
  - the book jacket cover for hardback books. Keeping the dust jacket on the book can preserve the visual interest as well as retaining the information found on the flaps and back of the jacket. If you are not worried about the visual interest, but would still like to retain the information, a cheaper option is to cut the flaps off the jacket and glue them to the inside of the covers.
  - laminate plastic for paperbacks. Both types of covers are available in a number of varieties and sizes and can be purchased as pre-cut sheets or on rolls.
- Cases for non-book items—These can either be the responsibility of the cataloging department or the department housing the item. If the latter, labels and the barcode will be sent with the item for application in the housing department. If the former, a number of cases will need to be kept on hand. CDs and DVDs can be kept in the case they come in or moved to new packaging. This depends on the security system used by the library and the durability of the originally packaging. There is also special packaging for mixed media, such as a book with multiple CDs. A sticker can be added that gives the number items for easy identification at check-in. Empty slots/pockets may also be marked. For non-standard-sized items, there are a variety of bags and plastic

boxes available. Again, exactly what is used is based on the item in hand and storage available.

- Date due slips and card pockets—These items are becoming less and less common, but are still in use by some libraries.
- Writing call number on the item—This is done so that if the spine label is removed, the call number is still known. Because of the ease of finding the call number in the online catalog, this step is often skipped. The call number may also be written on a slip of paper so that when the spine label is attached, it is easy to verify that the correct spine label is being put on the correct book.
- Spine labels—This step is almost always done after cataloging because once a cataloger looks at a record downloaded at the time of acquisitions, there might be some need to change to the call number or the record might not have any call number at all. Care and consideration should go into choosing spine labels and label printers. If subpar labels are used, they can easily fall off or be pulled off. For these reasons, many libraries also choose to use label protectors. The printer and ink are important because if the ink does not adhere well or has a tendency to fade, there will be a lot of added time and expense to replace the labels. Along with the call number label, there are a number of other identifying labels that can be placed on the spine. These can indicate age-level, format, topic, collection, or genre. Other labels can indicate non-standard circulation periods and circulation status (usually reference items or other items that cannot be checked out). These are often put on the inside or outside of the back cover.

Final Check

After all of the cataloging and processing is done, there is a step called *final check*. This step is preferably done by someone who has not previously worked on the items, but can be done by anyone. Having someone who has not previously worked on the items means that the records and items will be looked at with "fresh eyes" so it is more likely that errors will be caught, whereas someone who has worked on the items is more likely to see what he or she thinks should be there, rather than what is actually there.

The basic steps are:

- Bring up item by barcode
- Check that the correct item record/bibliographic record comes up
- Check that the call number on the item record and spine label match
- Check that the location code and status are correct
- Check that all of the physical processing has been done
- If applicable, check that anti-theft materials have been sensitized. (This step could be done by Circulation staff instead.)

To catalog is to follow cataloging standards and practices, but to make materials ready for patrons requires additional steps that will be unique to each library. Copy cataloging can save the time of the cataloger, and the three options suggested, or some combination of the second two (Z39.50 and vendors), will likely provide the basis of the work the cataloger does. Processing items is an additional step that cannot be ignored, simply because, to paraphrase Ranganathan, the father of Indian librarianship, items are meant for use. Processing is what ultimately permits that use by allowing items to be shelved, retrieved, checked out, and protected.

CONCLUSION

This book has shown how to catalog materials as a means of providing access through online retrieval systems such as ILSs. Cataloging is incredibly rewarding work, putting the cataloger squarely in the position of information intermediary in today's self-service, on-demand information retrieval environment.

When done correctly, cataloging can unfortunately be taken for granted. As you have seen, if humans are not able to input the metadata, surrogates will not be found and items, especially electronic ones or ones not in open-stack environments, will languish. Carefully curated and maintained collections are worth nothing if they cannot be consulted!

Cataloging correctly gives the power to the patron and can put local or less common materials in the same set of results as ones from publishing moguls cataloged by LC. When local or otherwise unique materials stand toe to toe with mass-produced materials collected by the world's leading libraries in terms of retrieval, the local catalogers have done their job. As the world shrinks thanks to advances in technology, the library has an increased role in bringing to the fore information, via standards-based surrogates, that otherwise would be lost in the sea of content.

NOTES

1. Cathy Blackman, Erica Rae Moore, Michelle Seikel, & Mandi Smith. 2014. "WorldCat and SkyRiver: A Comparison of Record Quantity and Fullness." *Library Resources & Technical Services* 58(3): 178–186.
2. Further information on downloading records from the Library of Congress and a list of other Z39.50 accessible catalogs can be found at http://www.loc.gov/z3950/.

SUGGESTED RESOURCE

American Library Association. 2014, October. "How to Acquire Cataloging Tools." *ALA Library Fact Sheet 18* www.ala.org/tools/libfactsheets/alalibraryfactsheet18

APPENDIX A

Examples of RDA Cataloging Records in MARC

Sometimes it is helpful to see some straightforward examples. The point of this appendix is to do just that. We have provided examples based on materials cataloged by the Library of Congress and analyzed by us. The formatting we use is based on examples provided by the Joint Steering Committee (JSC) (http://www.rdatoolkit.org/examples/MARC) to provide consistency. Each record appears twice, emphasizing a different standard.

The first record, the MARC record, shows the MARC tag, the indicators, and the encoded content. We use $ as the delimiter. We also provide a column to explain the meaning of the three-digit MARC tag; this should save you some time in looking it up.

In the second set of records presented, we carry out the descriptive cataloging of the same materials and cite the RDA instructions as we go. When comparing the RDA record with the previous MARC record for the item, you will note that there are some differences, as MARC and pure RDA have different requirements.

The core (i.e., required) fields, per RDA, are in white. These are fields that must be included in valid RDA records. The fields with a medium bit of gray are RDA fields that were not required, but that were included in these records by LC as a way of providing additional access. Classification numbers have also been included even though they are not really a part of RDA. The National Library of Australia, however, has a policy statement to use Identifier for the Item (RDA 2.20) to record the classification number, and we have used it here. Finally, content shaded more darkly gray is content that has not yet been developed in RDA. Subject and genre headings have been included here, although the subject portion of RDA has not yet been written (see placeholders in RDA sections 4 and 7).

Both sets of records go beyond basic or core cataloging—and represent a level of cataloging that we recommend. In some instances, optional or alternative instructions were used, and are explained in the notes. We hope that these records will help you make sense of what the final product of your cataloging endeavor will look like and will guide you in implementing what we have been describing in the previous ten chapters.

MARC RECORD EXAMPLES

Table A.1 MARC Record: Print Book—Adult Fiction (See Also RDA Record on Page 133 of This Book)

MARC Tag	MARC Field	Indicators	Data Recorded
Leader/06	Type of record		a
Leader/07	Bibliographic level		m
Leader/18	Descriptive cataloging form		i
Leader/19	Multipart resource record level		#[1]
007/00	Physical Description Fixed Field—Category of material		t
008/35–37	Fixed-Length Data Elements— Language		eng
020	International Standard Book Number	##[1]	$a 9781594747151 $q (hardcover)
020	International Standard Book Number	##	$a 1594747156 $q (hardcover)
040	Cataloging Source— Description conventions	##	$e rda
050	Library of Congress Call Number	00	$a PS3604.O3419 $b W555 2013
082	Dewey Decimal Classification Number	04	$a 812/.6 $2 23
100	Main Entry-Personal Name	1#	$a Doescher, Ian, $e author.
245	Title Statement	10	$a William Shakespeare's The Empire striketh back : $b Star wars part the fifth / $c by Ian Doescher ; inspired by the work of George Lucas and William Shakespeare.
246	Varying Form of Title	30	$a Empire striketh back
246	Varying Form of Title	30	$a Star wars part the fifth
264	Production, Publication, Distribution, Manufacture, and Copyright Notice	#1	$a Philadelphia : $b Quirk Books, $c [2014]
264	Production, Publication, Distribution, Manufacture, and Copyright Notice	#4	$c ©2014
300	Physical Description	##	$a 172 pages : $b illustrations ; $c 21 cm
336	Content Type	##	$a text $b txt $2 rdacontent
337	Media Type	##	$a unmediated $b n $2 rdamedia
338	Carrier Type	##	$a volume $b nc $2rdacarrier
500	General Note	##	$a "Lucas Books."

(Continued)

MARC Tag	MARC Field	Indicators	Data Recorded
520	Summary, Etc.	##	$a A retelling of The Empire strikes back in iambic pentameter, the style of Shakespeare. Many a fortnight have passed since the destruction of the Death Star, and the evil Darth Vader has hatched a plan to capture the rebels. Will Lord Vader learn how sharper than a tauntaun's tooth it is to have a Jedi child?
630	Subject Added Entry-Uniform Title	00	$a Empire strikes back (Motion picture) $v Adaptations.
600	Subject Added Entry-Personal Name	10	$a Shakespeare, William, $d 1564–1616 $v Parodies, imitations, etc.
650	Subject Added Entry–Topical Term	#0	$a Star Wars films $v Parodies, imitations, etc.
650	Subject Added Entry–Topical Term	#0	$a Star Wars fiction.[4]
655	Index Term-Genre/Form	#7	$a Science fiction. $2 lcgft
700	Added Entry-Personal Name	1#	$a Lucas, George, $d 1944–

Table A.2 MARC Record: Print Book—Adult Nonfiction (See Also RDA Record on Page 135 of This Book)

MARC Tag	MARC Field	Indicators	Data Recorded
Leader/06	Type of record		a
Leader/07	Bibliographic level		m
Leader/18	Descriptive cataloging form		i
Leader/19	Multipart resource record level		#[1]
007/00	Physical Description Fixed Field—Category of material		t
008/35–37	Fixed-Length Data Elements— Language		eng
020	International Standard Book Number	##[1]	$a 9780300190335 $q (hardback)
020	International Standard Book Number	##	$a 0300190336 $q (hardback)
040	Cataloging Source— Description conventions	##	$e rda
050	Library of Congress Call Number	00	$a BS1303 $b. S27 2014
082	Dewey Decimal Classification Number	00	$a 222/.32077 $2 23
130	Main Entry-Uniform Title	0#	$a Bible. $p Judges, I-XII, $l English. $s Sasson. $f 2014.
245	Title Statement	10	$a Judges 1–12 : $b a new translation with introduction and commentary / $c Jack M. Sasson.
264	Production, Publication, Distribution, Manufacture, and Copyright Notice	#1	$a New Haven [Connecticut] : $b Yale University Press, $c [2014]
264	Production, Publication, Distribution, Manufacture, and Copyright Notice	#4	$c ©2014
300	Physical Description	##	$a xx, 593 pages ; $c 24 cm.
336	Content Type	##	$a text $b txt $2 rdacontent
337	Media Type	##	$a unmediated $b n $2 rdamedia
338	Carrier Type	##	$a volume $b nc $2rdacarrier
490	Series Statement	1#	$a The Anchor Yale Bible ; $v volume 6D
504	Bibliography, Etc. Note	##	$a Includes bibliographical references and index.

(Continued)

Table A.2 (Continued)

MARC Tag	MARC Field	Indicators	Data Recorded
505	Formatted Contents Note	0#	$a Introduction. The rest in a commentary ; The book Judges ; The label of judges ; The texts of judges ; The assessment of judges ; The book of Judges in contemporary liturgy ; The study of Judges in the modern era ; This Anchor Yale Bible Judges — Bibliography — Translation — Notes and comments : prelude. The southern tribes ; The northern tribes — Notes and comments : arguments. What went wrong — Notes and comments : the judges. Othniel (Judg 3:7–11) ; Ehud (Judg 3:12–31) ; Deborah ; Gideon ; Abimelech ; "Minor" judges, major rift (Judg 10:17–11:28) ; Jephthah.
520	Summary, Etc.	##	$a "Informed by the cultures of the ancient world, this fresh translation and insightful commentary to chapters 1 to 12 of the biblical book of Judges provide a multilayered analysis of some of Scripture's most stirring narratives and verses. It expands understanding of the Hebrew text by explaining its meaning, exploring its contexts, and charting its effect over time. A comprehensive Introduction surveys issues and approaches in the study of Judges. Introductory Remarks identify issues of religious, social, cultural, or historical significance for most segments. These provide a background to the Notes and frame for the exposition in the concluding Comments"—$c Provided by publisher.
630	Subject Added Entry-Uniform Title	00	$a Bible. $p Judges $v Commentaries.
700	Added Entry-Personal Name	1#	$a Sasson, Jack M., $e author, $e translator.
830	Series Added Entry-Uniform Title	#0	$a Bible. $l English. $s Anchor Yale Bible. $f 2008 ; $v v. 6D.

Table A.3 MARC Record: Board Book—Children's Fiction (See Also RDA Record on Page 137 of This Book)

MARC Tag	MARC Field	Indicators	Data Recorded
Leader/06	Type of record		a
Leader/07	Bibliographic level		m
Leader/18	Descriptive cataloging form		i
Leader/19	Multipart resource record level		#[1]
007/00	Physical Description Fixed Field—Category of material		t
008/35–37	Fixed-Length Data Elements—Language		eng
020	International Standard Book Number	##[1]	$a 9780385374088
020	International Standard Book Number	##	$a 0385374089
040	Cataloging Source—Description Conventions	##	$e rda
050	Library of Congress Call Number	00	$a PZ8.3.S9223 $b Fas 2014
082	Dewey Decimal Classification Number	04	$a [E] $2 23
100	Main Entry—Personal Name	1#	$a Stubbs, Tommy, $e illustrator.
245	Title Statement	10	$a Fast train, slow train / $c illustrated by Tommy Stubbs.
250	Edition Statement	##	$a Abridged edition.
264	Production, Publication, Distribution, Manufacture, and Copyright Notice	#1	$a New York : $b Random House Children's Books, $c [2014]
264	Production, Publication, Distribution, Manufacture, and Copyright Notice	#4	$c ©2014
300	Physical Description	##	$a 1 volume (unpaged) : $b color illustrations ; $c 19 cm.
336	Content Type	##	$a text $b txt $2 rdacontent
336	Content Type	##	$a still image $b sti $2 rdacontent
337	Media Type	##	$a unmediated $b n $2 rdamedia
338	Carrier Type	##	$a volume $b nc $2rdacarrier

(*Continued*)

Table A.3 (Continued)

MARC Tag	MARC Field	Indicators	Data Recorded
490	Series Statement	1#	$a Big bright and early board books
500	General Note	##	$a "Thomas the Tank Engine & Friends created by Britt Allcroft, based on The Railway Series by The Reverend W. Awdry"—Back cover.
500	General Note	##	$a "This is an abridged edition of a work originally published in hardcover by Random House Children's Books in 2009"—Back cover.
500	General Note	##	$a On board pages.
520	Summary, Etc.	##	$a In this version of the "Tortoise and the Hare" fable, two train engines compete in a race.
650	Subject Added Entry–Topical Term	#0	$a Thomas the Tank Engine (Fictitious character) $v Juvenile fiction.
650	Subject Added Entry–Topical Term	#0	$a Railroad trains $v Juvenile fiction.
650	Subject Added Entry–Topical Term	#0	$a Racing $v Juvenile fiction.
650	Subject Added Entry–Topical Term	#0	$a Pride and vanity $v Juvenile fiction.
650	Subject Added Entry–Topical Term	#0	$a Board books.[4]
655	Index Term-Genre/Form	#7	$a Stories in rhyme. $2 lcgft
700	Added Entry—Personal Name	1#	$a Awdry, W. $t Railway series.
730	Added Entry—Uniform Title	0#	$a Thomas the tank engine and friends.
830	Series Added Entry—Uniform Title	#0	$a Big bright and early board books.

Table A.4 MARC Record: ebook—Adult Nonfiction (See Also RDA Record on Page 139 of This Book)

MARC Tag	MARC Field	Indicators	Data Recorded
Leader/06	Type of record		a
Leader/07	Bibliographic level		m
Leader/18	Descriptive cataloging form		i
Leader/19	Multipart resource Record		#[1]
007/00	Physical Description Fixed Field—Category of material		c
007/01	Physical Description Fixed Field—Specific material designation		r
007/03	Physical Description Fixed Field—Color		b
007/04	Physical Description Fixed Field—Dimensions		n
008/35–37	Fixed-Length Data Elements—Language		eng
020	International Standard Book Number	##[1]	$a 978456123789
040	Cataloging Source—Description conventions	##	$e rda
050	Library of Congress Call Number	14	$a DA690.W28 $b W55 2015
082	Dewey Decimal Classification Number	04	$a 942.7/19 $2 23
100	Main Entry—Personal Name	1#	$a Williams, Jane, $e author.
245	Title Statement	12	$a A history of the Unitary Authority of Warrington / $c by Jane Williams.
264	Production, Publication, Distribution, Manufacture, and Copyright Notice	#1	$a Cheshire, England : $b Goliath Publishers, $c 2015.
300	Physical Description	##	$a 1 online resource (xvii, 415 pages) : $b illustrations
336	Content Type	##	$a text $b txt $2 rdacontent
337	Media Type	##	$a computer $b c $2 rdamedia
338	Carrier Type	##	$a online resource $b cr $2 rdacarrier
504	Bibliography, Etc. Note	##	$a Includes bibliographical references (pages 405–409) and index.
588	Source of Description Note	##	$a Description based on print version record.
651	Subject Added Entry–Geographic Name	#0	$a Warrington (England) $x History.
776	Additional Physical Form Entry	08	$i Print version: $a Williams, Jane, author. $t A history of the Unitary Authority of Warrington $z 978123789456
856	Electronic Location and Access	40	$z http://goliath-merchandising.myshopify.com/

Table A.5 MARC Record: DVD—Feature Film (See Also RDA Record on Page 140 of This Book)

MARC Tag	MARC Field	Indicators	Data Recorded
Leader/06	Type of record		g
Leader/07	Bibliographic level		m
Leader/18	Descriptive cataloging form		i
Leader/19	Multipart resource record level		a
007/00	Physical Description Fixed Field—Category of material		v
007/01	Physical Description Fixed Field—Specific material designation		d
007/03	Physical Description Fixed Field—Color		c
007/04	Physical Description Fixed Field—Videorecording format		v
007/05	Physical Description Fixed Field—Sound on medium or separate		a
007/06	Physical Description Fixed Field—Medium for sound		i
008/35–37	Fixed-Length Data Elements—Language		eng
020	International Standard Book Number	##[1]	$a 9781594442258
024	Other Standard Identifier—Universal Product Code	1#	$a 796019795760
028	Publisher Number—Videorecording number	42	$a 79576 $b Weinstein Company
040	Cataloging Source—Description conventions	##	$e rda
041	Language Code	1#	$a eng $j eng $j spa
043	Geographic Area Code	##	$a e-uk-en
050	Library of Congress Call Number	04	$a PN1997.2 $b. G38 2006
082	Dewey Decimal Classification Number	04	$a 791.43 $2 23
245	Title Statement	04	$a The gathering / $c Granada Film presents in association with the Isle of Man Film Commission a Samuelson Productions and Granada Film production ; original screenplay by Anthony Horowitz ; produced by Marc Samuelson, Peter Samuelson, Pippa Cross ; directed by Brian Gilbert.
250	Edition Statement	##	$a Widescreen version.

MARC Tag	MARC Field	Indicators	Data Recorded
257	Country of Producing Entity	##	$a Great Britain
264	Production, Publication, Distribution, Manufacture, and Copyright Notice	#1	$a Santa Monica, Ca. : $b Designed, manufactured and distributed by Genius Products, $c [2006]
264	Production, Publication, Distribution, Manufacture, and Copyright Notice	#4	$c ©2006
300	Physical Description	##	$a 1 videodisc (87 min.) : $b sound, color ; $c 4 3/4 in.
336	Content Type	##	$a two-dimensional moving image $b tdi $2 rdacontent
337	Media Type	##	$a video $b v $2 rdamedia
338	Carrier Type	##	$a videodisc $b vd $2 rdacarrier
344	Sound Characteristics	##	$a digital $b optical $h Dolby Digital
346	Video Characteristics	##	$a laser optical
347	Digital File Characteristics	##	$a video file $b DVD video $e region 1
500	General Note	##	$a Dolby Digital; 5:1; widescreen
508	Creation/Production Credits Note	##	$a Editor, Mashahiro Hirakubo ; director of photography, Martin Fuhrer ; executive producers, Steve Christian, Jerome Gary, Anthony Horowitz, Patrick McKenna, Duncan Reid.
511	Cast Note	1#	$a Christina Ricci, Ioan Gruffudd, Stephen Dillane, Kerry Fox, Simon Russell Beale.
520	Summary, Etc.	##	$a An American backpacker's life takes a turn for the worse after a car accident in rural England.
538	System Details Note	##	$a DVD video; region 1.
546	Language Note	##	$a English; optional English or Spanish subtitles; closed captioning.
650	Subject Added Entry–Topical Term	#0	$a Backpacking $z England $v Drama.
650	Subject Added Entry–Topical Term	#0	$a Traffic accidents $z England $v Drama.
655	Index Term—Genre/Form	#7	$a Feature films. $2 lcgft
655	Index Term—Genre/Form	#7	$a Fiction films. $2 lcgft
655	Index Term—Genre/Form	#7	$a Thrillers (Motion pictures) $2 lcgft
700	Added Entry—Personal Name	1#	$a Horowitz, Anthony, $d 1955– $e screenwriter.

(*Continued*)

Table A.5 (Continued)

MARC Tag	MARC Field	Indicators	Data Recorded
700	Added Entry—Personal Name	1#	$a Samuelson, Marc, $d 1961– $e film producer.
700	Added Entry—Personal Name	1#	$a Samuelson, Peter, $d 1951– $e film producer.
700	Added Entry—Personal Name	1#	$a Cross, Pippa, $e film producer.
700	Added Entry—Personal Name	1#	$a Gilbert, Brian, $e film director.
700	Added Entry—Personal Name	1#	$a Ricci, Christina, $e actor.
700	Added Entry—Personal Name	1#	$a Gruffudd, Ioan, $e actor.
700	Added Entry—Personal Name	1#	$a Dillane, Stephen, $e actor.
710	Added Entry—Corporate Name	2#	$a Granada Films, $e presenter, $e production company.
710	Added Entry—Corporate Name	2#	$a Isle of Man Film Commission, $e presenter.
710	Added Entry—Corporate Name	2#	$a Samuelson Productions, $e production company.
710	Added Entry—Corporate Name	2#	$a Genius Products, LLC, $e video distributer.

Table A.6 MARC Record: CD—Music (See Also RDA Record on Page 143 of This Book)

MARC Tag	MARC Field	Indicators	Data Recorded
Leader/06	Type of record		j
Leader/07	Bibliographic level		m
Leader/18	Descriptive cataloging form		i
Leader/19	Multipart resource record level		#[1]
007/00	Physical Description Fixed Field—Category of material		s
007/01	Physical Description Fixed Field—Specific material designation		d
007/04	Physical Description Fixed Field—Configuration of playback channels		s
007/06	Physical Description Fixed Field—Dimensions		g
007/12	Physical Description Fixed Field—Special playback characteristics		e
007/13	Physical Description Fixed Field—Capture and storage technique		d
008/35–37	Fixed-Length Data Elements—Language		eng
028	Publisher Number—Issue number	02	$a 669447004417 $b Gotee Records
040	Cataloging Source—Description conventions		$e rda
050	Library of Congress Call Number	04	$a M2198.F56 $b F56 2013
082	Dewey Decimal Classification Number	04	$a 782.25/16408827 $2 23
110	Main Entry—Corporate Name	2#[1]	$a Finding Favour (Musical group)
245	Title Statement	10	$a Finding Favour.
264	Production, Publication, Distribution, Manufacture, and Copyright Notice	#1[2]	$a [United States] : $b Gotee Records, $c [2013]
264	Production, Publication, Distribution, Manufacture, and Copyright Notice	#2[3]	$a New York, NY : $b Columbia Records
264	Production, Publication, Distribution, Manufacture, and Copyright Notice	#4	$c ℗2013
300	Physical Description	##	$a 1 audio disc ; $c 4 3/4 in.
336	Content Type	##	$a performed music $b prm $2 rdacontent
337	Media Type	##	$a audio $b s $2 rdamedia

(*Continued*)

Table A.6 (Continued)

MARC Tag	MARC Field	Indicators	Data Recorded
338	Carrier Type	##	$a audio disc $b sd $2 rdacarrier
344	Sound Characteristics	##	$a digital $b optical $g stereo
347	Digital File Characteristics	##	$a audio file $b CD audio
505	Formatted Contents Note	0#	$a Shake the world — Love stepped in — Slip on by — Hallelujah we shall rise — Hero — I am.
650	Subject Added Entry–Topical Term	#0[4]	$a Christian rock music.
655	Index Term—Genre/Form	#7	$a Contemporary Christian music. $2 lcgft

Table A.7 MARC Record: Serial (See Also RDA Record on Page 144 of This Book)

MARC Tag	MARC Field	Indi-cators	Data Recorded
Leader/06	Type of record		a
Leader/07	Bibliographic record		s
Leader/18	Descriptive cataloging form		i
Leader/19	Multipart resource record level		#[1]
007/00	Physical Description Fixed Field—Category of material		t
008/35–37	Fixed-Length Data Elements—Language		eng
022	International Standard Serial Number	0#[1]	$a 2331–7639
040	Cataloging Source—Description conventions		$e rda
050	Library of Congress Call Number	00	$a TL1 $b. S5
082	Dewey Decimal Classification Number	10	$a 629 $2 23
130	Main Entry-Uniform Title	0#	$a Automotive engineering (2014)
222	Key Title	#0	$a Automotive engineering $b (2014, Print)
245	Title Statement	10	$a Automotive engineering.
264	Production, Publication, Distribution, Manufacture, and Copyright Notice	#1	$a Warrendale, PA : $b SAE International, $c [2014]-
300	Physical Description	##	$a volumes : $b color illustrations ; $c 28 cm
310	Current Publication Frequency	##	$a Eight issues per year
336	Content Type	##	$a text $b txt $2 rdacontent
337	Media Type	##	$a unmediated $b n $2 rdamedia
338	Carrier Type	##	$a volume $b nc $2 rdacarrier
362	Dates of Publication and/or Sequential Designation	1#	$a Began with Volume 1, Number 1 (February 4, 2014).
588	Source of Description Note	##	$a Description based on: Volume 1, Number 1 (February 4, 2014); title from cover.
588	Source of Description Note	##	$a Latest issue consulted: Volume 1, Number 2 (March 4, 2014).
650	Subject Added Entry—Topical Term	#0	$a Automobiles $x Design and construction $v Periodicals.
650	Subject Added Entry—Topical Term	#0	$a Trucks $x Design and construction $v Periodicals.

(Continued)

Table A.7 (Continued)

MARC Tag	MARC Field	Indi-cators	Data Recorded
710	Added Entry—Corporate Name	2#	$a Society of Automotive Engineers, $e author.
776	Additional Physical Form Entry	08	$i Online version: $t Automotive engineering (2014) $x 2331–7647 $w (DLC) 2013203886
780	Preceding Entry	00	$t Automotive engineering international $x 1543–849X $w (DLC) 98642389

RDA RECORD EXAMPLES

Table A.8 RDA Record: Print Book—Adult Fiction (See Also MARC Record on Page 119 of This Book)

RDA Instruction Number	RDA Element	Data Recorded
2.3.2	Title Proper	William Shakespeare's The Empire striketh back
2.3.4	Other Title Information	Star wars part the fifth
2.3.6	Variant Title	Empire striketh back
2.3.6	Variant Title	Star wars part the fifth
2.4.2	Statement of Responsibility Relating to Title Proper	by Ian Doescher
2.4.2	Statement of Responsibility Relating to Title Proper	inspired by the work of George Lucas and William Shakespeare
2.8.2	Place of Publication	Philadelphia
2.8.4	Publisher's Name	Quirk Books
2.8.6	Date of Publication	[2014]
2.11	Copyright Date	©2014
2.13	Mode of Issuance	single unit
2.15	Identifier for the Manifestation	9781594747151 (hardcover)
2.15	Identifier for the Manifestation	1594747156 (hardcover)
2.20	Identifier for the Item	PS3604.O3419 W555 2013
2.20	Identifier for the Item	812.6
3.2	Media Type	unmediated
3.3	Carrier Type	volume
3.4	Extent of Text	172 pages
3.5	Dimensions	21 cm
6.9	Content Type	text
7.10	Summarization of Content	A retelling of The Empire strikes back in iambic pentameter, the style of Shakespeare. Many a fortnight have passed since the destruction of the Death Star, and the evil Darth Vader has hatched a plan to capture the rebels. Will Lord Vader learn how sharper than a tauntaun's tooth it is to have a Jedi child?
7.15	Illustrative Content	illustrations
17.8	Work Manifested[5]	Doescher, Ian. William Shakespeare's The Empire Striketh Back

(Continued)

Table A.8 (Continued)

RDA Instruction Number	RDA Element	Data Recorded
19.2	Creator	Doescher, Ian
18.5	Relationship Designator	author
19.3	Other Person, Family, or Corporate Body Associated with a Work[6]	Lucas, George, 1944–
	Subject Heading—Guidelines Not Yet in RDA	Empire strikes back (Motion picture)—Adaptations
	Subject Heading—Guidelines Not Yet in RDA	Shakespeare, William, 1564–1616—Parodies, imitations, etc.
	Subject Heading—Guidelines Not Yet in RDA	Star Wars films—Parodies, imitations, etc.
	Subject Heading—Guidelines Not Yet in RDA	Star Wars fiction[4]
	Genre Heading—Guidelines Not Yet in RDA	Science fiction

Table A.9 RDA Record: Print Book—Adult Nonfiction (See Also MARC Record on Page 121 of This Book)

RDA Instruction Number	RDA Element	Data Recorded
2.3.2	Title Proper	Judges 1–12
2.3.4	Other Title Information	a new translation with introduction and commentary
2.4.2	Statement of Responsibility Relating to Title Proper	Jack M. Sasson
2.8.2	Place of Publication	New Haven [Connecticut]
2.8.4	Publisher's Name	Yale University Press
2.8.6	Date of Publication	[2014]
2.11	Copyright Date	©2014
2.12.2	Title Proper of Series	The Anchor Yale Bible
2.12.9	Numbering within Series	volume 6D
2.13	Mode of Issuance	single unit
2.15	Identifier for the Manifestation	9780300190335 (hardback)
2.15	Identifier for the Manifestation	0300190336 (hardback)
2.20	Identifier for the Item	BS1303. S27 2014
2.20	Identifier for the Item	222/.32077
3.2	Media Type	unmediated
3.3	Carrier Type	volume
3.4	Extent of Text	xx, 593 pages
3.5	Dimensions	24 cm
6.2.2	Preferred Title for the Work	Bible. Judges, I-XII. English. Sasson. 2014
6.9	Content Type	text
7.10	Summarization of Content	"Informed by the cultures of the ancient world, this fresh translation and insightful commentary to chapters 1 to 12 of the biblical book of Judges provide a multilayered analysis of some of Scripture's most stirring narratives and verses. It expands understanding of the Hebrew text by explaining its meaning, exploring its contexts, and charting its effect over time. A comprehensive Introduction surveys issues and approaches in the study of Judges. Introductory Remarks identify issues of religious, social, cultural, or historical significance for most segments. These provide a background to the Notes and frame for the exposition in the concluding Comments"—Provided by publisher

(Continued)

Table A.9 (Continued)

RDA Instruction Number	RDA Element	Data Recorded
7.16	Supplementary Content	Includes bibliographical references and index
17.8	Work Manifested[5]	Bible. Judges, I-XII, English. Sasson. 2014
19.2	Creator	Sasson, Jack M.
18.5	Relationship Designator	translator
18.5	Relationship Designator	author
25.1	Related Work	In series: Bible. English. Anchor Yale Bible. 2008
24.6	Numbering of Part	v. 6D
24.5	Relationship Designator	in series (work)
25.1	Related Work	Container of: Introduction. The rest in a commentary ; The book Judges ; The label of Judges ; The texts of Judges ; The assessment of Judges ; The book of Judges in contemporary liturgy ; The study of Judges in the modern era ; This Anchor Yale Bible Judges — Bibliography — Translation — Notes and comments : prelude. The southern tribes ; The northern tribes — Notes and comments : arguments. What went wrong — Notes and comments : the judges. Othniel (Jugd 3:7–11) ; Ehud (Judg 3:12–31) ; Deborah ; Gideon ; Abimelech ; "Minor" judges, major rift (Judg 10:17–11:28) ; Jephthah.
	Subject Heading—Guidelines Not Yet in RDA	Bible. Judges—Commentaries

Table A.10 RDA Record: Board Book—Children's Fiction (See Also MARC Record on Page 123 of This Book)

RDA Instruction Number	RDA Element	Data Recorded
2.3.2	Title Proper	Fast train, slow train
2.4.2	Statement of Responsibility Relating to Title Proper	illustrated by Tommy Stubbs
2.5.2	Designation of Edition	Abridged edition
2.8.2	Place of Publication	New York
2.8.4	Publisher's Name	Random House Children's Books
2.8.6	Date of Publication	[2014]
2.11	Copyright Date	©2014
2.12.2	Title Proper of Series	Big bright and early board books
2.13	Mode of Issuance	single unit
2.15	Identifier for the Manifestation	9780385374088
2.15	Identifier for the Manifestation	0385374089
2.20	Identifier for the Item	PZ8.3.S9223 Fas 2014
2.20	Identifier for the Item	[E]
3.2	Media Type	unmediated
3.3	Carrier Type	volume
3.4	Extent of Text	1 volume (unpaged)
3.5	Dimensions	19 cm
6.9	Content Type	text
6.9	Content Type	still image
7.10	Summarization of the Content	In this version of the "Tortoise and the Hare" fable, two train engines compete in a race.
7.15	Illustrative Content[7]	illustrations
7.17	Colour Content[8]	color
17.8	Work Manifested[5]	Stubbs, Tommy. Fast train, slow train
20.2	Contributor	Stubbs, Tommy
18.5	Relationship Designator	illustrator
24.4.3	Description of The Related Work, Expression, Manifestation, or Item[9]	"This is an abridged edition of a work originally published in hardcover by Random house Children's Books in 2009"—Back cover
25.1	Related Work[10]	Big bright and early board books

(Continued)

Table A.10   (Continued)

RDA Instruction Number	RDA Element	Data Recorded
24.5	Relationship Designator	in series (work)
25.1	Related Work[10]	Based on: Awdry, W. Railway series.
25.1	Related Work[10]	Thomas the tank engine and friends.
25.1	Related Work [11]	"Thomas the Tank Engine & Friends created by Britt Allcroft, based on The Railway Series by The Reverend W. Awdry"—Back cover
	Subject Heading—Guidelines Not Yet in RDA	Thomas the Tank Engine (Fictitious character)—Juvenile fiction
	Subject Heading—Guidelines Not Yet in RDA	Railroad trains—Juvenile fiction
	Subject Heading—Guidelines Not Yet in RDA	Racing—Juvenile fiction
	Subject Heading—Guidelines Not Yet in RDA	Pride and vanity—Juvenile fiction
	Subject Heading—Guidelines Not Yet in RDA	Board books[4]
	Genre Heading—Guidelines Not Yet in RDA	Stories in rhyme

Table A.11 RDA Record: ebook—Adult Nonfiction (See Also MARC Record on Page 125 of This Book)

RDA Instruction Number	RDA Element	Data Recorded
2.3.2	Title Proper	A history of the Unitary Authority of Warrington
2.4.2	Statement of Responsibility Relating to Title Proper	by Jane Williams
2.8.2	Place of Publication	Cheshire, England
2.8.4	Publisher's Name	Goliath Publishers
2.8.6	Date of Publication	2015
2.13	Mode of Issuance	single unit
2.15	Identifier for the Manifestation	ISBN 978456123789
2.17.13	Note on Issue, Part, or Iteration Used as the Basis for Identification of the Resource	Description based on print version record
2.20	Identifier for the Item	DA690.W28 W55 2015
2.20	Identifier for the Item	942.7/19
3.2	Media Type	computer
3.3	Carrier Type	online resource
3.4	Extent of Text	1 online resource (xvii, 415 pages)
4.6	Uniform Resource Identifier[12]	http://goliath-merchandising.myshopify.com/
6.9	Content Type	text
7.15	Illustrative Content	illustrations
7.16	Supplementary Content	Includes bibliographical references (pages 405–409) and index
17.8	Work Manifested[5]	Williams, Jane. History of the Unitary Authority of Warrington
19.2	Creator	Williams, Jane
18.5	Relationship Designator	author
27.1	Related Manifestation[13]	Print version: A history of the Unitary Authority of Warrington / by Jane Williams—978123789456
27.1	Related Manifestation	ISBN 978123789456
	Subject Heading—Guidelines Not Yet in RDA	Warrington (England)—History

Table A.12 RDA Record: DVD—Feature Film (See Also MARC Record on Page 126 of This Book)

RDA Instruction Number	RDA Element	Data Recorded
2.3.2	Title Proper	The gathering
2.4.2	Statement of Responsibility Relating to Title Proper	Granada Film presents in association with the Isle of Man Film Commission a Samuelson Productions and Granada Film production
2.4.2	Statement of Responsibility Relating to Title Proper	original screenplay by Anthony Horowitz
2.4.2	Statement of Responsibility Relating to Title Proper	produced by Marc Samuelson, Peter Samuelson, Pippa Cross
2.4.2	Statement of Responsibility Relating to Title Proper	directed by Brian Gilbert
2.5.2	Designation of Edition	Widescreen version
2.8.2	Place of Publication	Santa Monica, Ca.
2.8.4	Publisher's Name	Designed, manufactured and distributed by Genius Products
2.8.6	Date of Publication	[2006]
2.11	Copyright Date	©2006
2.13	Mode of Issuance	single unit
2.15	Identifier for the Manifestation	ISBN: 9781594442258
2.15	Identifier for the Manifestation[14]	UPC: 796019795760
2.15	Identifier for the Manifestation[14]	Weinstein Company : 79576
2.20	Identifier for the Item	PN1997.2. G38 2006
2.20	Identifier for the Item	791.43
3.2	Media Type	video
3.3	Carrier Type	videodisc
3.4	Extent	1 videodisc
3.5	Dimensions	4 3/4 in.
3.16.2	Type of Recording	digital
3.16.3	Recording Medium	optical
3.16.9	Special Playback Characteristic	Dolby Digital, 5:1
3.18.2	Video Format	laser optical
3.19.2	Digital File Type	video file
3.19.3	Encoding Format	DVD video
3.19.6	Regional Encoding	Region 1

RDA Instruction Number	RDA Element	Data Recorded
6.9	Content Type	two-dimensional moving image
7.10	Summarization of Content	An American backpacker's life takes a turn for the worse after a car accident in rural England
7.12	Language of the Content	English; optional English or Spanish subtitles
7.14	Accessibility Content	Closed captioning in English
7.17.3	Colour of Moving Image	color
7.18	Sound Content	sound
7.19	Aspect Ratio	widescreen
7.22	Duration	87 min.
7.23	Performer, Narrator, and/or Presenter	Cast: Christina Ricci, Ioan Gruffudd, Stephen Dillane, Kerry Fox, Simon Russell Beale
7.24	Artistic and/or Technical Credit	Credits: editor, Mashahiro Hirakubo ; director of photography, Martin Fuhrer ; executive producers, Steve Christian, Jerome Gary, Anthony Horowitz, Patrick McKenna, Duncan Reid
17.8	Work Manifested[5]	Gathering (Motion picture)
19.2	Creator	Horowitz, Anthony, 1955–
18.5	Relationship Designator	screenwriter
19.3	Other Person, Family, or Corporate Body Associated with a Work	Samuelson, Marc, 1961–
18.5	Relationship Designator	film producer
19.3	Other Person, Family, or Corporate Body Associated with a Work	Samuelson, Peter, 1951–
18.5	Relationship Designator	film producer
19.3	Other Person, Family, or Corporate Body Associated with a Work	Cross, Pippa
18.5	Relationship Designator	film producer
19.3	Other Person, Family, or Corporate Body Associated with a Work	Gilbert, Brian
18.5	Relationship Designator	film director
20.2	Contributor	Ricci, Christina
18.5	Relationship Designator	actor
20.2	Contributor	Gruffudd, Ioan
18.5	Relationship Designator	Actor
20.2	Contributor	Dillane, Stephen

(Continued)

141

RDA Instruction Number	RDA Element	Data Recorded
18.5	Relationship Designator	actor
19.3	Other Person, Family, or Corporate Body Associated with a Work	Granada Films
18.5	Relationship Designator	presenter
18.5	Relationship Designator	production company
20.2	Contributor	Isle of Man Film Commission
18.5	Relationship Designator	presenter
19.3	Other Person, Family, or Corporate Body Associated with a Work	Samuelson Productions
18.5	Relationship designator	production company
21.4	Distributor	Genius Products, LLC
	Subject Heading—Guidelines Not Yet in RDA	Backpacking—England—Drama
	Subject Heading—Guidelines Not Yet in RDA	Traffic accidents—England—Drama
	Genre Heading—Guidelines Not Yet in RDA	Feature films
	Genre Heading—Guidelines Not Yet in RDA	Fiction films
	Genre Heading—Guidelines Not Yet in RDA	Thrillers (Motion pictures)

Table A.13 RDA Record: CD—Music (See Also MARC Record on Page 129 of This Book)

RDA Instruction Number	RDA Element	Data Recorded
2.3.2	Title Proper	Finding Favour
2.8.2	Place of Publication	[United States]
2.8.4	Publisher's Name	Gotee Records
2.8.6	Date of Publication	[2013]
2.9.2	Place of Distribution	New York, NY
2.9.4	Distributor's Name	Columbia Records
2.11	Copyright Date	℗2013
2.13	Mode of Issuance	single unit
2.15	Identifier for the Manifestation	Gotee Records: 669447004417
2.20	Identifier for the Item	M2198.F56 F56 2013
2.20	Identifier for the Item	782.25/16408827
3.2	Media Type	audio
3.3	Carrier Type	audio disc
3.4	Extent	1 audio disc
3.5	Dimensions[15]	4 3/4 in.
3.16.2	Type of Recording	digital
3.16.3	Recording Medium	optical
3.16.8	Configuration of Playback Channels	stereo
3.19.2	Digital File Type	audio file
3.19.3	Encoding Format	CD audio
6.9	Content Type	performed music
7.12	Language of the Content	In English
17.8	Work Manifested[5]	Finding Favour (Musical group). Finding Favour
19.2	Creator	Finding Favour (Musical group)
18.5	Relationship Designator	performer
25.1	Related Work	Container of: Shake the world — Love stepped in — Slip on by — Hallelujah we shall rise — Hero — I am
	Subject Heading—Guidelines Not Yet in RDA	Christian rock music[4]
	Genre Heading—Guidelines Not Yet in RDA	Contemporary Christian music

Table A.14 RDA Record: Serial (See Also MARC Record on Page 131 of This Book)

RDA Instruction Number	RDA Element	Data Recorded
2.3.2	Title Proper	Automotive engineering
2.3.9	Key Title	Automotive engineering (2014, Print)
2.6.2	Numeric and/or Alphabetic Designation of First Issue or Part of Sequence	Volume 1, Number 1
2.6.3	Chronological Designation of First Issue or Part of Sequence	February 4, 2014
2.8.2	Place of Publication	Warrendale, PA
2.8.4	Publisher's Name	SAE International
2.8.6	Date of Publication	[2014]-
2.13	Mode of Issuance	serial
2.15	Identifier for the Manifestation	ISSN 2331–7639
2.17.2.3	Title Source	Title from cover
2.17.12	Note on Frequency	Eight issues per year
2.17.13	Note on Issue, Part, or Iteration Used as the Basis for Identification of the Resource[12]	Description based on: Volume 1, Number 1 (February 4, 2014)
2.17.13	Note on Issue, Part, or Iteration Used as the Basis for Identification of the Resource[12]	Latest issue consulted: Volume 1, Number 2 (March 4, 2014)
2.20	Identifier for the Item	TL1. S5
2.20	Identifier for the Item	629
3.2	Media Type	unmediated
3.3	Carrier Type	volume
3.4	Extent	volumes
3.5	Dimensions	28 cm
6.2.2	Preferred Title for the Work	Automotive engineering
6.4	Date of Work	2014
6.9	Content Type	text
7.12	Language of the Content	in English
7.15	Illustrative Content	illustrations
7.17	Colour Content	color
17.8	Work Manifested[5]	Automotive engineering (2014)
21.3	Publisher	Society of Automotive Engineers
25.1	Related Work	Automotive engineering international
24.5	Relationship Designator	continues (work)

RDA Instruction Number	RDA Element	Data Recorded
27.1	Related Manifestation[13]	Online version: Automotive engineering (2014)
27.1	Related Manifestation	ISSN: 2331–7647
	Subject Heading—Guidelines Not Yet in RDA	Automobiles—Design and construction—Periodicals
	Subject Heading—Guidelines Not Yet in RDA	Trucks—Design and construction—Periodicals

NOTES

1. # indicates that no content is supplied by the cataloger/field is left blank.
2. Function of entity: Publication.
3. Function of entity: Distribution.
4. No genre term equivalent.
5. No equivalent encoding in MARC 21.
6. Other person, family, or corporate body associated with a work is a core element if the access point representing that person, family, or corporate body is used to construct the authorized access point representing the work (see 6.27–6.31).
7. LC-PCC PS: *LC practice*: Illustrative content is a core element for LC for resources intended for children.
8. LC-PCC PS: *LC practice*: Use the spelling "color" when recording that term.
9. Recorded using an unstructured description.
10. Related work recorded using an authorized access point representing the related work.
11. Unstructured Description of the Related Work.
12. Core element for LC/PCC.
13. Related manifestation recorded using a structured description and an identifier.
14. If there is more than one identifier for the manifestation, prefer an internationally recognized identifier, if applicable. Additional identifiers for the manifestation are optional.
15. LC-PCC PS for 3.5.1.1.1 Discs: LC practice: Record the diameter of discs in inches.

APPENDIX B

Cataloging Tools: A Bibliography/Webliography

WEB-BASED CATALOGING RESOURCES: FREELY AVAILABLE

Cataloging calculator. http://calculate.alptown.com/

Classify: An Experimental Classification Web Service. http://classify.oclc.org/classify2/

Dublin Core Metadata Initiative. http://dublincore.org

Library of Congress authorities. http://authorities.loc.gov

About Library of Congress authorities. http://authorities.loc.gov/help/contents.htm

See "Searching" and "Search results" on left-hand menu

Library of Congress Classification schedules. http://www.loc.gov/aba/cataloging/classification/

Library of Congress online catalog. http://catalog.loc.gov

Library of Congress Subject Headings and Genre/Form Terms. http://www.loc.gov/aba/cataloging/subject/

Library of Congress. Network Development and MARC Standards Office. 2004. *MARC 21 Concise Format for Bibliographic Data.* Retrieved from http://www.loc.gov/marc/bibliographic/ecbdhome.html

LTI. 2009. *What Is Authority Control?* http://www.librarytech.com/A-AINT-B.html

OCLC Bibliographic Formats and Standards. http://www.oclc.org/bibformats

Tillett, Barbara. 2004. *What Is FRBR? : A Conceptual Model for the Bibliographic Universe. http://www.loc.gov/cds/downloads/FRBR.PDF*

WorldCat. http://www.worldcat.org/

Z39.50. http://www.loc.gov/z3950/agency/

WEB-BASED CATALOGING RESOURCES: SUBSCRIPTION PRODUCTS

Cataloger's Desktop. http://www.loc.gov/cds/desktop/

Classification Web. https://classificationweb.net/

OCLC Connexion. http://connexion.oclc.org/

RDA Toolkit. http://access.rdatoolkit.org/

WebDewey. http://connexion.oclc.org/

BIBLIOGRAPHY

General Cataloging Textbook

Joudrey, Daniel N., Arlene G. Taylor, and David P. Miller. 2015. *Introduction to Cataloging and Classification.* 11th ed. Santa Barbara, CA: Libraries Unlimited.

Cataloging with RDA

(Many of these resources assume a prior knowledge of cataloging and AACR2.)

El-Sherbini, Magda. 2013. *RDA: Strategies for Implementation.* Chicago: ALA Editions.

Hart, Amy. 2014. *RDA Made Simple: A Practical Guide to the New Cataloging Rules.* Santa Barbara, CA: Libraries Unlimited.

Intner, Sheila S., and Jean Weihs. 2014. *Standard Cataloging for School and Public Libraries.* 5th ed. Santa Barbara, CA: Libraries Unlimited.

Kincy, Chamya Pompey and Sara Shatford Layne. 2014. *Making the Move to RDA: A Self-Study Primer for Catalogers.* Lanham, MD: Rowman & Littlefield Publishers.

Library of Congress (LC) RDA Training Materials. n.d. http://www.loc.gov/catwork shop/RDA%20training%20materials/LC%20RDA%20Training/LC%20RDA%20 course%20table.html

Maxwell, Robert L. 2014. *Maxwell's Handbook for RDA: Explaining and Illustrating RDA, Resource Description and Access Using MARC 21.* Chicago: ALA Editions.

Mering, Margaret, ed. 2014. *The RDA Workbook: Learning the Basics of Resource Description and Access.* Santa Barbara, CA: Libraries Unlimited.

Oliver, Chris. 2010. *Introducing RDA: A Guide to the Basics.* Chicago: ALA Editions.

School Library Cataloging Resources

Intner, Sheila S., and Jean Weihs. 2014. *Standard Cataloging for School and Public Libraries.* 5th ed. Santa Barbara, CA: Libraries Unlimited.

Intner, Sheila S., Joanna F. Fountain, and Jean Weihs, eds. 2011. *Cataloging Correctly for Kids: An Introduction to the Tools*. 5th ed. Chicago: American Library Association.

Miller, Joseph, ed. 2007. *Sears List of Subject Headings*. 19th ed. New York: H.W. Wilson. Retrieved from http://support.epnet.com/uploads/kb/sears_19th_edition.pdf. Please note this is an old edition.

Print Versions of Cataloging Resources

Bristow, Barbara A., ed. 2014. *Sears List of Subject Headings*. 21st ed. Ipswich, MA: H.W. Wilson.

Cutter, Charles Ammi. 1969. *Cutter-Sanborn Three Figure Author Table*. Chicopee, MA: H.R. Huntting Co.

Mitchell, Joan S., ed. 2011. *Dewey Decimal Classification and Relative Index*. 4 vol. 23rd ed. Dublin, OH: OCLC Online Computer Library Center, Inc.

Mitchell, Joan S., ed. 2012. *Abridged Dewey Decimal Classification and Relative Index*. 15th ed. Dublin, OH: OCLC Online Computer Library Center, Inc.

Scholarly and Professional Journals

Cataloging and Classification Quarterly (CCQ)
Cataloging Service Bulletin (CSB)
International Cataloguing and Bibliographic Control (ICBC)
Library Resources & Technical Services (LRTS)
Library Technology Reports
Technical Services Quarterly (Tech Serv Q)

Clarifying Cataloging Jargon

The ODLIS (*Online Dictionary for Library and Information Science*) by Joan M. Reitz (http://www.abc-clio.com/ODLIS/odlis_A.aspx) is a great resource when the vocabulary being used in the cataloging literature is otherwise inscrutable.

APPENDIX C

Professional Resources
for Catalogers

There are a number of resources and training opportunities available for catalogers. They range from beginner to advanced and can be general introductions or on a specific format or type of material.

ALCTS

The Association for Library Collections and Technical Services (ALCTS) (pronounced *-uh-lex*) is a division of the American Library Association (ALA). ALCTS is further subdivided into sections. The section most applicable to catalogers is the Cataloging and Metadata Management section (CaMMs) (previously known as the Cataloging and Classification Section [CCS]). The Continuing Resources Section (CRS) also provides cataloging training and information. Below the section level, there are a number of interest groups and committees that focus on a particular aspect of cataloging. ALCTS offers webinars, some free and some not (their free ones can be found on their YouTube channel, https://www.youtube.com/user/alctsce/), "Fundamentals" series of web courses for various aspects of technical services, and preconference sessions and programs at ALA Annual and Midwinter.

WEBINARS AND OTHER TRAINING MATERIALS

In addition to ALCTS, a number of other groups offer web-based training. The RDA Toolkit offers a free Toolkit Essentials live webinar (http://www.rdatoolkit.org/training) every two to three months, with the archived versions available at all times. The Library of Congress makes all of their training materials available online, for free. They also have the Catalogers Learning Workshop (CLW) (http://www.loc.gov/catworkshop/) that provides information on all aspects of cataloging. These training materials are a mix of PDF documents, webinar/video presentations, and in-person trainings. Amigos Library Services, MARC of Quality, and Midwest Collaborative for Library Services also offer online training opportunities. Many states also have associations, consortia, or other groups that offer training opportunities, both online and in-person.

Additional Cataloging Support/Continuing Education

- Cataloguing Section of IFLA (International Federation of Library Associations and Institutions) http://www.ifla.org/cataloguing; http://archive.ifla.org/VII/s13/
- Library of Congress Workshop Course Materials http://www.loc.gov/catworkshop/courses/index.html
- Library of Congress Cataloging Distribution Service http://www.loc.gov/cds/
- Library of Congress Cataloging Tools, Documentation http://www.loc.gov/aba/cataloging/tools/
- NISO National Information Standards Organization http://www.niso.org/home/

EMAIL DISTRIBUTION LISTS AND OTHER ONLINE MEDIA

There are a number of email distribution lists for catalogers. The most popular is AutoCat. AutoCat is for all things concerning cataloging. Users can pose questions about specific problems on any aspect of cataloging, classification, or physical processing of items. There are also discussions/information about cataloging policies and theory, job announcements, and training opportunities. Another listserv is RDA-L. This listserv is specifically for questions and discussion about RDA. OCLC-CAT is for users of any of OCLC's cataloging and metadata services. Users of other products should check with the company responsible to see if there is a listserv. Groups like OLAC (Online Audiovisual Catalogers, Inc.) and the Music Library Association (MLA) also have email distribution lists, although they are usually broader in nature, so non-cataloging topics are discussed. Many state library associations and consortia also offer email distribution lists, which may or may not have lists dedicated solely to cataloging.

High-quality content is also freely available on the web and through social media. Blogs, for example, can be another source of cataloging information. Some blogs are "official" and run by companies or groups associated in some way with cataloging. Others are musings of catalogers, with varying amounts of cataloging knowledge and experience. There are too many to list here, but Planet Cataloging (http://planetcataloging.org/) is an aggregator for cataloging blogs. YouTube can also be a source of cataloging training or provide information relevant to cataloging. As with the blogs, the videos found here come from a number of sources, so one should be careful when using them. Finally, information about cataloging is shared on Twitter and other social media outlets such as the Facebook pages for various associations. With Twitter in particular, though, not only are there announcements made about materials and events of interest to catalogers, but it is also possible to ask and have answered questions about cataloging. As with the other information on the web, it is important to vet content for accuracy.

Email Distribution Lists

- AutoCat http://listserv.syr.edu/scripts/wa.exe?SUBED1=autocat&A=1
- BIBFRAME (Bibliographic Framework Transition Initiative Forum) http://listserv.loc .gov/listarch/bibframe.html
- NGC4Lib (Next Generation Catalogs for Libraries) http://dewey.library.nd.edu/ mailing-lists/ngc4lib/
- OCLC-CAT is a discussion forum for library staff using or considering any OCLC cataloging and metadata services. http://listserv.oclc.org/archives/oclc-cat.html
- RDA-L: http://www.lsoft.com/scripts/wl.exe?SL1=RDA-L&H=LISTSERV.LAC-BAC .GC.CA

INDEX

ABOUT THE AUTHORS

Heather Lea Moulaison, PhD, is assistant professor at the iSchool at the University of Missouri in Columbia. She has been working and researching in Information Organization (IO) since 2002 when she first began professional work as a cataloging librarian. Since that time, she has taught cataloging in three countries on two continents and continues to explore research and instruction in IO topics such as metadata and organization in archives. Moulaison is the coeditor of a LITA book on cloud computing and coauthor of a book on digital preservation for the LAM community. Active in the library community, she was elected to ALA Council as a councilor-at-large for 2014–2017 and has also been elected internationally to the governing body of the Association Internationale Francophone des Bibliothécaires et Documentalistes (AIFBD), the international Francophone library association.

Raegan Wiechert, MLS, is assistant professor and cataloger at Missouri State University. A cataloging librarian with 10 years' experience, Wiechert has co-taught numerous sections of MSU's LIS 508/608 and 7312 Principles of Cataloging and Classification through the cooperative agreement with the University of Missouri's LIS program. Additionally, she has given countless seminars on RDA cataloging throughout the state of Missouri for the MOBIUS Consortium and serves as the chair of her cluster's Cataloging Committee. Nationally, Wiechert has done service for the Association for Library Collections & Technical Services (ALCTS)'s Cataloging and Metadata Management Section (CaMMS) and the ALCTS Cataloging and Classification Section (CCS); she also served on the ALCTS Task Force on Competencies & Education for a Career in Cataloging.

CPSIA information can be obtained
at www.ICGtesting.com
Printed in the USA
FFHW010048150719
53592384-59274FF